CW00497380

THE ANA
OF HATE

Revati Laul is an independent journalist and activist. She started her career in television with NDTV, then shifted to print, writing for publications like *Tehelka*, *The Quint* and the *Hindustan Times*. As an outcome of her work on political violence, she created the Sarfaroshi Foundation in the district of Shamli in Uttar Pradesh, where she now lives. This is her first book.

Praise for *The Anatomy of Hate*

'Laul does not offer us a morality tale. She does not write fiction. She tells us, in eloquent prose and careful detail, the stories of the life trajectories of these three very different men who participated in the mass hate crimes of 2002. By so doing, she holds a mirror to us as a people: to who we are, what we have become, and what we can become. Their stories must concern us, if we are to both understand and hopefully one day end hate violence. This is a rare book, brave and fiercely honest, unsettling, deeply troubling. Those who worry about the future of India cannot afford to miss it.'

– Harsh Mander, *The Hindu*

'Laul attempts to present each of the individuals and organisations in a nuanced light—be it the VHP, the Congress, the RSS, or the BJP. Like all serious books on serious subjects, it doesn't answer all the questions, but Laul challenges the reader to read more on and around it. The book sets a robust standard for journalistic non-fiction in India.'

– Rahul Jayaram, *Scroll.in*

'Besides its beautifully crafted beginning and end, Laul's book has an extraordinary middle, too, that holds important lessons for India's future. The middle is when the violence deep inside these people and societies begins to morph.'

– Seema Chishti, *The Indian Express*

'*The Anatomy of Hate* is an important contribution to our understanding of the political role of hate, rage, anger, violence and, of course, love. It is also an important exploration of the crucial link between the individual and the collective psyche ... [B]ringing the two together, as Laul does in this book, can offer constructive avenues of engaging with the politics of "othering" and work towards building better relations between communities.'

– Rakesh Shukla, *Himal Southasaian*

THE
ANATOMY
OF HATE

REVATI LAUL

cntxt

First published in hardback by Context, an imprint of Westland Publications Private Limited, in 2018

First published in paperback in 2023 by Context, an imprint of Westland Books, a division of Nasadiya Technologies Private Limited

No. 269/2B, First Floor, 'Irai Arul', Vimalraj Street, Nethaji Nagar, Alapakkam Main Road, Maduravoyal, Chennai 600095

Westland, the Westland logo, Context and the Context logo are the trademarks of Nasadiya Technologies Private Limited, or its affiliates.

ISBN: 9789395073578

10 9 8 7 6 5 4 3 2 1

Typeset by SŪRYA, New Delhi
Printed at Parksons Graphics Pvt Ltd

*To my mother,
my everything*

'Ujaaley mein khada insaan dekh nahin sakta; jo andherey mein khada hai, usko dikh jaata hai sab.'

(Brightness is blinding. It's when you're standing in the dark that you really begin to see.)

—Farida Bano Abdul Qadir Khalifa, witness and survivor of the Naroda Patiya massacre in Ahmedabad, Gujarat, 2002, on being questioned in court about her ability to identify members of the mob in the night.

THE TWENTY-EIGHTH

ONE

Of all the signs telling Abdul Majid his world was about to crumble, the khichdi is the one that truly hit home. It was the middle of the afternoon on 28 February 2002 when the mob closed in on Naroda Patiya. Majid was hiding on a terrace when Jai Bhawani spotted him from below and went up to talk to him.

'Majidbhai,' he said, 'you guys have been hungry since the morning. Come down and bring me those large cooking vessels from your kitchen. I'll make some kadhi khichdi.'

Majid stood up suddenly. 'Kadhi khichdi? Kadhi khichdi! But that's food for a funeral,' he said, feeling a sudden surge of panic.

'Yes,' Jai Bhawani replied. 'You are all going to die.'

Majid ran down the stairs. He had locked his wife and kids and mother-in-law in a temple right behind the house, where he assumed that Jai Bhawani would keep them safe. The friendly neighbour he thought he could trust.

Majid scrambled to let them out. They ran together. Separately. Then in broad daylight, everything went dark. Majid lay in a heap near Teesra Kuan, the Third Well, struck in the back of his head by what felt like a sword. As he was fading in and out of consciousness, he heard his daughter calling out to him from the nearby park. 'Abba, abbaaaaa ...' By the time he came to, her body was cold.

He had lost six children, his pregnant wife and mother-in-law. Looking back, Majid counted the signs he had missed the day before.

There had been signs. At the street corner, away from the screeching buses on the main road, Majid had overheard traders and autorickshaw drivers discuss the possibility of violence erupting in this part of Ahmedabad. Revenge, he heard, was spreading its tentacles across the state of Gujarat after fifty-nine Hindu volunteers from the Vishwa Hindu Parishad, or VHP, the World Hindu Council, were burnt alive on a train. The bogey they were in had caught fire in a Muslim-majority town called Godhra. Some said that was so far away—130 kilometres, a two-and-a-half-hour bus ride from the industrial wasteland of Naroda Patiya. Even though this was also a Muslim neighbourhood, Majid thought it was too insignificant to matter. But then he thought about the fact that Hindus had been killed. What if they decided it was time to teach Muslims everywhere a lesson? If Majid was unsure of how to read the signs, the afternoon news spelt it out in bold. A headline in the Gujarat paper *Sandesh*, being sold at the railway stall, screamed 'Khoon ka badla khoon'. Blood for blood.

Later that night, as Majid was downing the noisy metallic shutter to his grocery store, he had seen Jai Bhawani go past, lugging a heavy thirty-five-litre barrel with him.

'Is that alcohol you're carting home?' he had asked.

Jai Bhawani had said, 'No, Bhai. Actually, it's petrol.'

That certainly should have been an early warning sign. Why was he carrying so much fuel? Instead, it was the khichdi the next day that finally sank in. Bhawani and his friends killed Majid's family, tossed their bodies into Teesra Kuan, poured petrol and set them alight. 'They came prepared with snacks and drinks,' he remembered. Over fifteen years of telling, his narrative was now set in rigor mortis. There is a blankness to his description of how his mother-in-law's polyester sari had melted in the fire so that the two daughters who had clung to her—Afreen Bano and Shaheen Bano—were found stuck to the grandmother in their charred state.

ৱ

On that day, the mob had also encircled Kauser Bi near Teesra Kuan. She was pregnant and due any day, so she could not run. Her husband, Firozbhai, was stuck on the other side of the road, unable to cross because everything was blocked off by fire and an out-of-control mob. He only heard later, when he went to claim his wife's body, of how Suresh Langdo, Babu Bajrangi, Jai Bhawani and Guddu Chhara had surrounded her, murdered her, ripped out the foetus within her with a sword and killed it. He was sure of it, because of the state her body was found in, and also because her fourteen-year-old nephew Javed saw it while hiding under a pile of bodies, pretending to be dead. He described it in court eight years later.

Ever since, Firozbhai has been talking to Kauser Bi in his dreams. 'We were both exactly alike. One kind of people,' he said, looking back. He has been scattering flowers on her grave every year since then. Red roses. She had worn a lovely red salwar kameez on their wedding day.

ৱ

Among the survivors of the twenty-eighth was someone who took thirteen years to see herself as a victim. She did not lose her family that day. She was, in fact, married to a man from the mob. A man who had helped kill Abdul Majid's family and Kauser Bi. His name was Suresh Jadeja, better known in these parts as Suresh Langdo, the man with the bad leg.

The day before the violence, Suresh's wife had a fever. They were at the local doctor's when they heard about the burning of coach S6 of the Sabarmati Express. The coach was carrying Hindus, mostly from the VHP, returning from Uttar Pradesh where they had been on a religious campaign, when someone pulled the chain and the train stopped abruptly in the Muslim-majority town of Godhra. A fight had erupted at the railway station and then the train bogey was burned down.

The doctor's wife and daughter were on that train. They spoke of how lucky the two of them were to have not been in the compartment that had caught fire. Of the indelible scars they bore from the sights they had seen. Of the burned bodies and the stench. And the panic they felt as they ran for their lives.

As they left the clinic, Suresh's anger was rising. He turned to his wife and remarked, 'If it is those Muslims that have done this, I will not let them be.'

'Why can't you just see this as people being burned?' asked Suresh's wife, now scared for her life. Her name was Farzana Bano and she was Muslim.

They got home and Suresh started a heated conversation with his uncle and neighbour, Jayantibhai. 'You don't get mixed up in all of this. Just stick with your family, I'm telling you,' Jayantibhai said in a vain attempt to temper the conversation.

The next morning, Farzana went out to buy a bag of atta to make rotis for breakfast. It was a little after nine in the morning and most shops were either closed or shutting down for the day. The VHP had declared a lockdown, and no one was taking any chances. In the distance, Farzana saw a moving mass of people getting larger and larger. The shopkeeper was surprised to see her and said, 'Hurry up and leave! There's going to be trouble.' She ran back home and reported all of this to Suresh. 'You stay right here,' he said. 'I will go and see what's going on.' Farzana in turn instructed their two children not to leave the house, and went across to Suresh's chacha and chachi's place next door: his father's younger brother Jayantibhai and his wife, Radhaben. Everyone climbed up to the roof of Radhaben's dhaba for a better view of the action across the street. Farzana saw a soda bottle being lobbed at Suresh's younger brother, Raju, from across the road. It cut his forehead. Jayanti ran out to rescue his bleeding nephew.

Farzana had her eyes glued to the road. She saw her husband emerge with a long bamboo pole and smash an autorickshaw to bits, and just then she was distracted by a group of Muslim schoolgirls who had run in their direction, seeking shelter from the mob. They had their Qurans clasped close to their chests as they ran into Jayantibhai's house, thirsty, out of breath and scared. Farzana reckoned they had gone to the nearby madrasa for their early-morning Quran class. They must be about nine she thought, roughly the same age as her daughter Richie* who was safe at home next door. Farzana scrambled off the roof with Radhaben to calm the girls down. They sat there till three in the afternoon when Suresh returned, his shirt soaked in sweat. He was starting to say to Farzana—'So many people have died, many were burnt'—when he spotted the girls seated there. 'They should all be cut to pieces,' he erupted. But it was his chacha's house

* All names marked with an asterisk have been changed to conceal the identity of the person.

and he couldn't do much. Jayantibhai quickly packed the girls off to the State Reserve Police quarters across the boundary wall for safekeeping.

Suresh turned to Farzana now with a completely different expression. 'Go put on an extra-large red tilak on your forehead now, understood?' The concerned husband, worried that his Muslim wife would be singled out. She was Muslim second, wife first. Once he was done instructing her, Suresh went out to re-join the mob.

A few hours later, Farzana saw an exodus from her gully. People were making their way across the road in a steady stream, and coming back with loot from abandoned homes. Televisions, fridges and, at the very least, large brassware and steel cooking pots. She couldn't remain indoors in the midst of all of this; she had to see what was going on. Farzana followed the crowd until she saw something that caused her to stop abruptly and turn back. A head stuck in the wheel of an abandoned bicycle. A head without a body.

२

Ten-year-old Guddu* had the same impulse as Farzana. He tried hard to blot out the inferno from the street with *Agneepath*, which was being telecast on TV. A film that starred his favourite actor, Amitabh Bachchan. But it did not work. He had also run out in the direction of the crowd till his eye stopped at an open window billowing with thick, grey smoke. It was the window of a small mud hut with a thatched roof. Inside it was the body of a burning woman tied to a pole. She was on fire, flames leaping up from her feet, her sari ablaze. Her eyes were open. There was no sound at all, her screams long snuffed out by death. But her eyes were fixed on him as he ran back home.

The images followed him like static. They would not let him sleep. He was sobbing uncontrollably, convinced that the carnage in the street was all his fault. His mother had told him not to step out of the house but he hadn't listened. The events of the day fused with a trauma from two years ago. His grandmother had asked him to lift an earthen matka of water lying at the other end of her room and put it by her bedside. But he had dropped it, scattering all the water and shattering the clay. Later that day, his grandmother had died and the elders gathered around had said, 'If Guddu hadn't smashed that matka, she would still be alive.'

ঽ

In an adjoining gully, Farzana was trying hard to contain her fear while also dealing with the excitement of Suresh's family who saw the day as an opportunity. Radhaben had just returned home fresh from the day's loot. She could not resist making a dig at Farzana for having run back. 'Such a coward. You should've gone further. It was something else, that sight,' she had said.

It wasn't until about 11.30 at night that Suresh got back home. He was pouring sweat, the smell abominable. Farzana cooked a basic dinner of tomato, onion subzi and rotis, during which he constantly reprimanded her for having stepped out at all. 'Can you not get it into your head that you could have been a target? The VHP people were also looking for you,' Suresh said angrily. 'They were saying there's a Muslim in my house. I told them that you are one of us now. You put a tikka on your forehead and all. They said okay. If it's actually like that, then we won't touch her.'

It was late and there was no electricity in the area. Farzana and Suresh were living in the tenement above Jayantibhai's house, since their own quarters were being reconstructed. Farzana lit a diya and they were settling in for the night when Suresh suggested that the children and she not sleep at home. That they move with his chacha–chachi and the rest of the neighbourhood to the open fields at the back in case any Muslims came looking for revenge. Most of their neighbours had decided not to sleep in their homes that night.

But first Suresh pulled Farzana back into the house and thrust himself on top of her. 'He was still stinking so much,' Farzana recalled with a grimace. She had turned her face away.

And heard him say, 'Achha, so now you don't want me anymore, haan?'

She replied, 'How can that even be possible? But now, in the middle of all of this also? What if we have to get out and run? If someone comes in, how will we run like this?'

After he was done, Suresh handed Farzana a dagger.

'I've never killed a fly, what do you want me to do with this?' she said to him.

'Shove it into the stomach of any Muslim who tries to approach you,' he replied.

As she stood there stupefied, there was the sound of laughter ringing in her ears. Suresh's family found it impossibly funny that Farzana had been handed a knife. She heard them use the pejorative term for Muslim. It stung sharply. 'Qajji! The Qajji is scared of a knife, ha ha ha!'

Suresh went back out. It was dark.

২

The mob had thinned to a slow trickle when Shaikh Moiuddin, who lived down the road, witnessed a scene he couldn't get out of his head. It was the sight of five-year-old

Nilofer, along with Shah Rukh and Shahzad, in the middle of a mob in the street below, her unmistakable bald pate bobbing up and down like a celebratory coconut. She was dancing with her friends and a few adults. The Hindu-owned dhabas had turned on some music from the blockbuster film that was playing in cinemas that week. *Kabhi Khushi Kabhie Gham*. Times of celebration, times of despair.

With such madness being unleashed upon this one street of Ahmedabad city, it was uncanny, thought Moiuddin, that the mob had spared the mad children. There they were—eating and drinking, entirely unaware of all that had happened.

TWO

In a hilly, corn-growing village far from the flames of Naroda Patiya, Dungar* felt a tightness in the air, as if a pressure cooker was on the boil. His broad face was heating up as rumours began to spread—did a train burn, what had the Muslims done? Some people said they had raped a Hindu girl in the neighbouring area. That last bit of gossip spread faster than anything else, because it was the worst possible thing to imagine. Dungar's small black eyes became slits, his large nose flared as he declared, 'I knew there was going to be a riot.' Looking back, he could see that the anger rising in him was a convenient outlet for long-held envy.

There was a part of Dungar that was always ashamed of not having a pucca house with a marble floor like the ones he had seen some Muslim traders build for themselves. On trips to the nearby town and farther out to big cities, as he watched people in fancy cars and airconditioned homes, the poison was slowly building up like a slow poison. How small and insignificant his life was. And how uncomfortable. Now was the chance for that long-suppressed rage to merge with the tidal wave sweeping across Gujarat. Anger with a purpose.

He was a member of the VHP. A Hindu revivalist group that was designed to harness anger. Especially the discontent of aspirational people like him, with no place for their dreams to grow. 'The ground had been prepared much before February 2002,' Dungar explained, his voice high-pitched. 'We were told again and again at meetings that Muslims belong in Pakistan. This is Hindustan. Hindustan is for Hindus. So something like this was bound to happen.' It felt good. Like something was finally moving. He wasn't sure how things would improve for him if Muslims were pushed out of the country, but for now there was something to soak up all his anger, and that was purpose enough.

Dungar's village was a long distance from Godhra. The hill slopes, with their thin forest cover, looked like a caravan of camels sleeping in the sun, their backs lined with bristly hair. The main road was some distance away, so people weren't plugged in to the news like they were in other parts of Gujarat. Electricity was in short supply and hardly anyone in the area owned a TV. Only half the inhabitants were literate, so newspapers were almost entirely absent, except as wrappers for tobacco or sweets. Rumours were the most immediate way for news to get around. They were like the local intoxicants that felt headier with each successive hit. That's the space in which an insider in the VHP, like Dungar, could play arbiter. The referee of rumours, standing at the local chai shop, hands on hips, chest out, his broad shoulders pushed back confidently as he held forth.

'We didn't know a train was going to be burnt. But our leaders were preparing us for the election that was going to take place later in the year. So people's minds had to be stuffed with something, na,' Dungar explained. Everything was building up to move the Bharatiya Janata Party—the BJP, an ally of the VHP—towards a win. 'Otherwise why were VHP people being taken in trains from Gujarat, for what?' Dungar asked, looking back on the propaganda campaign the VHP–BJP combine had driven. They had created a fictional account of long Hindu victimhood, telling Hindus everywhere they had to unite to save themselves from people and parties that appeased Muslims. The Hindu right said that the Congress party, which had been in power for six decades, favoured Muslims even though they made up only 14 per cent of the Indian population, because Hindus never voted as one bloc. Now it was time for the religious majority to consolidate. Hindus made up 80 per cent of the population. But so far, their votes had been stratified, each sub-group, caste and sub-caste had voted differently. Anger and an imagined oppressor were uniting them—and thus, potentially their votes—for the first time ever.

Dungar heard of how Hindus had been persecuted for centuries by Islamic despots like the medieval king Babur. That he built a mosque in the city of Ayodhya in Uttar Pradesh at the birthplace of the Hindu god Ram. It needed to be destroyed, and it was. The VHP's Ayodhya campaign led to the destruction of the Babri masjid in 1992. Ten years later, it was time for a second wave. For Hindus to rally around and build a temple at the site of the desecrated mosque. This was the campaign that the VHP volunteers had travelled on the train for. Now fifty-nine of them were dead. And as a VHP member, Dungar felt duty-bound to help the village figure out what to do next. It also gave him the validation he was looking for.

But this was also harvest season in corn-growing country. There was enough uncertainty to deal with. The silky beards on corn cobs had dried and turned purple, indicating that they were ripe for picking. The ones at the top of the stalk, facing the sun, had to be plucked immediately. Row by row, one cob at a time, everyone was counting their crop. And figuring out if they were sunk or would get a decent price in the market. Revenge for Hindus who died in Godhra was the farthest thing from their minds.

Still, Dungar had a mandate to fulfil. He was a member of the three main institutions that made up the Hindu right or the Sangh Parivar: the VHP that was populated by aspirational Hindus, the intellectual arm called the RSS or the Rashtriya Swayamsevak Sangh and the militant arm called the Bajrang Dal. If Dungar did not act, he would lose the credit built up over time. On the other hand, he had been raised to live in constant fear of the police. What if he acted against Muslims and got caught later? It was a tough call.

The Sangh had perhaps figured out his dilemma; it knew that this was a region where loyalty was proclaimed loudly but practised selectively. People would waver. So, the VHP's district head, who was also the elected representative of the BJP, called a meeting of all Sangh Parivar members. This man knew he had to send out a message to locally appointed leaders like Dungar that they were being watched.

At the meeting, Dungar was among a select gathering of troopers. Their leader was positioned in front of the temple dedicated to Lord Meghnad, the warrior god who fought Lord Ram. The leader towered over everyone in the village because of his political clout and booming voice, moustache twirled impressively. 'If, even on a day like this, you can't act against Muslims, then go home and put on some bangles,' he thundered to his audience of two hundred-odd men. 'You have one day,' he declared. 'Burn those Muslims.'

Dungar remembers the adrenaline rush. The leader's words were like a commandment. But once the speech was over and the crowds dispersed into little communal huddles to discuss the matter, it became a lot more complicated. Dungar was a Bhil, as were a significant number of people in his village. They were the largest tribal group in Gujarat, and had a century of oppression behind them, which made fear their singular driving force.

'My mind was drifting,' Dungar said, his forehead creased, eyebrows raised as he went back over the tentativeness of those days. 'I thought, what will these big leaders from the Sangh Parivar do later, a year from now. Will they abandon us?' It was hard for Dungar to trust the assurances of the Hindu leader. His family had settled into the relatively comfortable status of middling farmers with a few acres of land after two generations of migration from one part of Gujarat to another. Nothing had come easy. He had to balance his fear of the Sangh with his fear of the police. The resources and social status so carefully acquired over three generations of tactical manoeuvring could not be jeopardised for the sake of immediate but uncertain political gains. Shouting in solidarity was one thing; acting on it, quite another.

But he knew better than to let the concern show on his face. Dungar smiled to cover his anxiety. 'Sab theek, sab theek'—everything is okay, he said, like always. Especially because it was not. For the moment, he decided it was best to wait and watch. His scepticism was echoed by others in the village. Despite their leader's rousing speech, no one was convinced that they had to set anything or anyone on fire just yet. The provocation for that came a day later.

It was evening, and Dungar and his friends were sitting idly at the village bus station. It was nearly time for the evening's hooch from the tall, palm-shaped mahuda† trees when they saw Irfanbhai.* He was headed in their direction

---

† Mahuda is what the mahua tree (*Madhuca indica*) is called in Gujarat.

in a tempo-truck. Like the other Muslims in the village, he had fled with his family to an area with a predominantly Muslim population, where he could count on being protected. Since there had been no violence in the village so far, he was making a quick trip back to retrieve important items from his abandoned home.

As soon as he spotted Dungar and his friends, Irfan panicked. 'He must've thought we were going to attack him, even though we weren't. We were just sitting there,' Dungar clarified later. Irfan turned to his companion and whispered something. From where he was sitting, Dungar could not make out what was being said. But before he knew it, Irfan's companion had taken out a gun and fired in the air. Bam! Bàm! The audacity of it made Dungar's barely contained anger spiral out of control. That Muslims like Irfanbhai, who ought to be taught a lesson for the train burning, had actually taken it upon themselves to strike first was too much to bear. 'They were the ones who started it all,' Dungar emphasised. That evening, the tide turned. 'We decided to act,' he said.

The decision was unanimous and announced with a flourish. 'There will be no Muslims in our villages. No Muslims allowed!'

The next day, Dungar called everyone to a meeting at the Rama Pir temple. At that time, it occurred to no one that the temple dedicated to the fourteenth-century mystic was revered by both Muslims and Hindus. Now it was transformed into a site of twenty-first-century hate. After the gunshots, Dungar didn't need to say much. It was amply clear that all those who had come to the meeting were in on the plan. About forty people turned up to set fire to the twelve Muslim houses in the area. 'If any Muslim had actually crossed my path that day, I would have cut him to pieces and burnt his body,' Dungar said, looking back.

The action began the following night, on 2 March. A plan was drawn up. Dungar wanted to be as precise and careful as possible. Roads leading in to the village were blocked. Spindly babul trees were cut down, their barks laid across the road to block access to Muslims from neighbouring villages. The targeted homes were completely empty. But a strong message needed to be sent out: that the Muslims would not be able to return home.

'That day was all about maaro, kaato aur jalao—cut, kill and burn,' Dungar said. 'I wore my RSS chaddi and topi that time,' he added. The khakhi shorts and cap has been the RSS uniform since its inception in 1925, the design borrowed from the uniforms of Nazi soldiers fighting in Northern Africa during World War II. (It has recently gone through a redesign to gradually replace shorts with trousers.)

Dungar's friend Roop Sinh* was tasked with buying kerosene and petrol. Money was collected—Rs 10 or 20 a head from most households. From shopkeepers and those with a little more money, Rs 100 each. It was enough to buy the fuel needed for the job. Dungar divided the group of six main players into three teams, each of which had two houses to burn. Petrol and kerosene were poured from the barrels into individual pouches. They waited for it to get dark. The moon lent these empty homes a ghostly glow. Crickets were screeching from end to cornfield end. The villagers had emptied out into the jungle for the night amid rumours that the Muslims were coming back to attack them.

Dungar and Roop Sinh got into their vehicle, drove some distance, then proceeded quietly on foot. They had reached Islambhai's* house, which was made of tightly packed mud walls and a thatch roof. Dungar held a clutch of dried twigs he'd gathered from the season's tuar dal crop. He placed them onto the firewood already lying around the house. Roop poured kerosene on all of this and around the house, and struck a match. He added a generous dose of petrol and up it went in flames. The two-member teams copy-pasted this routine on all the homes they were assigned.

As the next roof caved in, and the next, Dungar found that burning down houses wasn't as simple task a task as he had imagined. 'I was beginning to fill up with regret. And I was very tired,' he recalled. As the houses burned, his mind roamed uncomfortably. To the times he had visited the grocery shops attached to these houses as a little boy, no money in hand, for a fistful of rice or a free toffee. There they were now—ash-grey frames against a mangled skyline, lit from the inside by burning embers. Sweets and rice charred and stuck to the floor. Of all the homes Dungar and his friends burnt over the next day and a half, it was the home of Parvez that he couldn't get out of his head. 'It was a large and beautiful blue-and-white house,' he remembered. Much bigger and better than his own thatch-roofed and mud-walled home. Haji Parvez's house, too, had an attached grocery store. It was stocked with tons of grain, dal and a brood of chickens. 'The whole thing burnt for seven days. Seven whole days!' Dungar remarked. The grain caught fire. The chickens shrieked. Dungar got home and sat down to dinner. His wife had made her usual brinjal concoction—a spicy ringan-nu-shaak—with corn rotis. He said nothing to her of what he had done. But the images of Parvez's house had burnt themselves into his brain and would not let him sleep. He sweated profusely, tossed and turned, still breathing in the thick, sharp smoke. And hearing the sound of the roof as it caved in—bhadaam!

The next morning, it was time for Dungar to revert to

his VHP avatar. As the Hindu organisation's local boss, he had to play his part. 'I went out with the group once again,' he recalled. 'And then we made plans for the next set of houses to burn.'

THREE

Revenge spread its tentacles across Gujarat, infecting the unlikeliest people. Like twenty-eight-year-old Pranav* sitting in his MA class in a large, green university campus. He was educated, English-speaking and from the new, rising middle class. He came from one of the most politically and socially dominant caste groups in the state. And everything about him was a study in contrasts. His accented English would have made another person self-conscious. Instead, there was a certain loftiness and ease built into Pranav's wiry frame. His eyes were fierce but his small jaw was locked into an ever-mocking cast. He was clearly not the kind of person to get mixed up in mob violence. Until now.

Pranav was in class when he first heard about the train burning and had no idea what all the fuss was about. The incident had happened in another town to other people. Why were his college mates suddenly so anxious? It was about 3.30 p.m. when various heads of department began to get frantic calls from the administration. Classes that were meant to go on until five started to wind up early. Pranav ran down to the parking lot with his hostel mates—his go-to gang for everything. Curiosity was getting the better of him. The hostel was right around the corner, but he and his friends were undecided. Should they get back to their rooms or hang out in college and try and find out what was going

on? They were sitting astride motorbikes weighing their
options when one of them spotted their head of department
walking out of the building.

'Haan, there may be trouble tomorrow,' is all they
managed to get out of him. Pranav wasn't sure what to make
of that warning, but he was struck by how worried the man
looked. 'I have to find a way of getting your new psychology
teacher to the railway station. She lives in the adjoining city
and she is Christian,' he told Pranav. Though the target of
the mob was Muslims, in the past, some of the Hindu right's
propaganda had also been anti-Christian. On a day like this,
nothing could be taken for granted.

Pranav thought about the route. Getting to the railway
station was scary; he'd have to cross a Muslim ghetto. But
he had been brought up to be afraid of nothing, the natural
sense of entitlement that came from caste privilege. His casual
appearance—an unironed shirt and rubber flip-flops—were
only one way of deflecting attention from an inner intensity
and compulsive need for control. He turned to his professor
and said, 'Theek hai, I'll drop her off.'

The town was eerily silent. Chai shops and vada pao
stands were closed. The streets, normally packed with
scooters, cycles and cars that out-shouted each other, were
deserted. Many spots along the way to the station could have
spelt trouble; especially the large Muslim tenements flanking
the railway line where the road turned into a river of sewage.
These spaces radiated fear to Pranav even on a normal day.
But his friends looked up to him, so he would rope them in
for a recce to take away some of the fear of venturing out
on a day like this.

His friends did pitch in. They did eight or ten rounds of
the town on their bikes and found a spot where volunteers

were escorting people to buses that were headed to the railway station. That is where Pranav decided it was safe to take his teacher. He steadied his nerves, sat the psychology teacher on his bike and drove there. When they arrived, a volunteer turned to him and said, 'Don't take any tension. We are from the VHP. And we're taking all Hindus safely.' Now Pranav was worried. He cautioned his teacher, 'Please don't tell anyone your name, ma'am.' It was a clearly identifiable Christian name. He relaxed only after news reached him that she was home safe.

Next, he had to find out if his parents were in danger. They lived in a village that was several hours by bus from his college. He called them from the hostel phone and was relieved to hear them say it was all quiet at home. By the end of the day, Pranav and his friends had assessed things better, and realised that they were in no direct danger. There was a Muslim colony two-and-a-half kilometres away, but their immediate surroundings were Hindu.

Since the town was in lockdown mode, everyone converged in Pranav's hostel room for the day's gossip. Soon, because it was the default hangout, a group of people from the local town also dropped by. They were armed with information that was precise and tactile. A full itinerary for the looting of Muslim shops and businesses around town, starting with details of where the action was going to be that night. 'Tonight, this is the shop that will be torn down,' they informed the college boys. 'If you want anything, come get it.'

In the beginning, the offer scared Pranav a little. What if they were part of the mob that went to watch the looting and the police picked them up as accomplices, he thought. This was followed by another, more lofty dismissal. 'I didn't want to wear stolen stuff,' he said. Some of his classmates did. They returned later that night, full of booty to display.

'Look at all these things we've got! This ... and also ... this!'

Pranav interjected, 'But what about the police? Weren't they there?'

His friends replied, 'Yes, they were. In fact, they were the ones telling us we have ten minutes to do what we want and then we have to leave. So we went in, burned the shop down and ran. After that, another lot of police vehicles arrived at the spot. By that time, it was understood that we could not be seen there anymore, or we'd get beaten up.'

There was a system in place.

'If the police are there, then what is there to worry about?' Pranav thought.

He decided to go along the following night. But he would do it his way. He would not take his own bike but ride pillion with a friend instead. He declared, as if he was the chief guest and the organisers needed to have their protocol in place, 'I will come but I am giving you my 100 per cent assurance that, if anything happens, I will not wait for you. Then don't turn around and tell me you need help with getting your bike out of there or anything. I will just run. And whatever happens, happens. If you still want to take me along, then okay.'

His friend assured Pranav that they would only circle the area and do no more. A strictly viewing-only enterprise.

With that clear, they set out. The plan that night was to pillage the Bata shoe shop. Everyone liked Bata shoes. It was a symbol of the old middle class, of school shoes, and now of a brand being left behind by Nike and Reebok. The brand represented childhood, cricket, relay races and, for many, their first ever pair of sports shoes. So it wasn't altogether clear what the excitement was about—revenge against Muslims or a shot at free shoes. Once they got to the venue, Pranav was relieved to see that his hostel mates had turned up in large numbers. He didn't grab shoes like the rest, but stood by and watched. And made a few customary digs at his mates. 'Are you beggars, all of you? Have you never seen shoes before or what?'

While he was taking in the sights and sounds, Pranav spotted a couple of policemen standing there. Deciding not to stay longer, he grabbed his friend and made a quick exit. Back in their dormitory, they settled in and waited for the others to return. They learnt that one of their hostel mates had not stuck to the plan. He arrived on the scene late to find that the lower storey of the shop had been emptied of shoes. So he had climbed up the loft to find a pair. By this time, the police on guard had gone, and the next lot had arrived to do the officially mandated duty of clearing the crime scene of whoever remained past the deadline. The boy's mates screamed out to him as he was hanging from the loft with a pair of shoes in hand—'Police, police!' The warning startled him. He crashed to the ground, breaking a leg. Later, he returned to the hostel limping, the butt of everyone's jokes. 'Go steal more Bata shoes!'

This was beginning to be fun. On most nights, Pranav would watch the action from the hostel terrace, part voyeur, part sceptic, watching his hostel mates join local Hindu leaders who were armed with gas cylinders. 'They would explode—phad, phad!' he recalled. 'And the shops used to burn right to the top.'

Thieving built up an appetite, and one night, Pranav's friends were particularly hungry. Since the usual midnight haunts were shut, someone suggested, why not ransack the neighbouring food shop? High on a series of shoplifts, his friends drew up a plan. As the details were being fleshed out, Pranav realised that the shop in question was owned by a Hindu. 'This'll kill us, guys. We'll end up with a police case,' he interrupted his friends to say.

'Who says we'll get caught? If someone asks us, we'll just say, how do we know who burnt the shop,' his friends replied. 'We can also say it was people from the Muslim village that did it. We told them not to.'

With that sorted out, four of Pranav's classmates pried open the shutter to the food shop with an iron rod. They ransacked the place of all the available food, then set it on fire. The following day, when they were asked if they knew what had happened, they said it was Muslims from the village nearby.

'Our general view of Muslims wasn't very positive,' Pranav remembered. 'We thought they were a bit dirty. And they did everything upside down.' He added, 'It wasn't like we wanted them to die or anything like that. We were just caught up in the swing of things and felt we weren't responsible for their fate.'

With phones barely accessible and national news often blocked out, information on what went on elsewhere came to Pranav most vividly through stories everyone told of goings-on in their respective hometowns.

'In our area toh we really beat them up well.'

'In ours they tied a guy between two bikes and drove them in different directions.'

'In my hometown they cut up fifteen or twenty of them.'

'All finished in our village. The end of them. Khallaas.'

What struck Pranav most when he looked back on those days was the pride with which these stories were told. It was a tidal wave that built on itself. Everyone was a part of it. Even the college department head seemed to validate the goings-on. It was endorsement, if any was needed for a sceptic like Pranav, to hear his head of department say, 'Whatever is happening is right.'

秀

The twenty-eighth was not a calendar day. It was a black hole that bent time. In the lives of Suresh, Dungar and Pranav, it re-arranged all previous days and experiences. There were always many choices to be made; what part of their identities to sharpen, what to suppress. Choice is a vexing word. What part of choice applies when a tidal wave of anger tears through a state? What part of it is the moment, the madness, the collective, and what part individual, personal history?

We will never know precisely. But once the day was done, the randomness of the individual actions of each of our three protagonists—Suresh, Dungar and Pranav—acquired a new purpose. It drew fresh lines from their pasts that were a complex mix of deliberate action and circumstance: their lives before they were the mob.

BEFORE

FOUR

Before you could see where Suresh came from, you smelled it. In the fumes of sour hooch that rose from big, blue plastic barrels in every house in the street. If you sniffed too closely, it burned the eyes. Pouches of this sharp glue-like substance were packed tightly in plastic. The packets were camouflaged with mud and refuse from the street, and lowered into barrels to be sold later by the women of the house. The substance was hidden from view in a city where selling and consuming liquor was prohibited by law. The law enforcers knew precisely where it was to be found, but preferred to look away and take a cut. It wasn't as if the rest of the city didn't drink. Liquor was stashed away in cupboards and consumed by polite people in other parts of Ahmedabad city, equally well hidden from the police. But the hooch sellers of Chharanagar were much more defiant. Liquor was an old trade handed down the generations. By the time Suresh was born, this tribe—once a nomadic group of small traders—had been branded as criminals going back a century.

So it was that Suresh grew up in the 1970s in a neighbourhood of professional criminals—thieves, smugglers and gamblers—men and women alike. They owed their notoriety to a law put in place in 1871 by the British. The colonisers were terrified of nomadic tribes like the Chharas and their constant movement, especially after the Great Revolt of 1857. So they labelled them 'criminal tribes', people who were 'addicted to the systematic commission of non-bailable offences'. All 150,000 Chharas were stuffed into internment camps, with a daily roll call and head count. Robbed of their traditional livelihood, the Chharas found that the only way they could now live was as outlaws.

In Suresh's time, being labelled the son of a thief had become a badge of honour. But in the same densely packed shanty, there were others who wore that badge very differently. The large and busy Kubernagar railway crossing ran across the outer perimeter of Chharanagar like a wire, cauterising the dingy interior from the rest of the city. One road led away from the railway line, past furniture shops and chicken lolly stands to Suresh's house. The other snaked past a clothing store with a big purple signboard—Rich Girl—right up to the house of Suresh's contemporary, Dakxin Chhara. Both were roughly the same age and grew up in the same zone, but with entirely different worlds in their heads. There were, in fact, so many nagars in Chharanagar.

For Dakxin too, the family history of thieving made for an exciting tale. His eyes danced as he said, 'My father's life was very dramatic.' His father was nicknamed Dagad Dev, or sharpshooter, a man who never missed his aim. As a child, Dagad threw stones at all kinds of targets—from fruit trees to people's heads. His indulgent mother decided to name him for it and it stuck. It was just as well he had such good aim, because on some days, fruit was all the family had to eat. In the Nandurbar area of Gujarat where Dagad was growing up, all he knew was grinding poverty and the incessant burning of an empty stomach. He was often out on the streets, beating his chest violently, begging passers-by to feed him. His flair for drama combined with some clever sleight of hand brought food home. It also gave Dagad the opportunity to move his family to Chharanagar, where others from their tribe lived.

One day, Dagad Dev was squatting in the common defecating ground, taking a collective dump with two others. They were having a heated exchange over some sort of numbers. Dagad was intrigued.

He interrupted them: 'Tell me what you're arguing over, maybe I can help.'

'No, you won't know anything,' the duo said dismissively.

But they were all still squatting, so Dagad Dev persisted. He hadn't earned his name for nothing. 'Try me,' he said and they let him in on their gambling business.

It turned out they were messing up their accounts and that Dagad was a genius with numbers. He outshone them in their business and, soon enough, was the godfather of the Chharanagar gamblers. By the end of his career, a hundred families owed their jobs and basic dal–roti to him in the mini-gambling units and allied businesses he had helped them set up. Dakxin declared proudly that his father was their lifeline.

Dagad Dev's exploits took him out of Chharanagar to tourist spots across the country—from Agra to Kanyakumari—where stealing from tourists was good business. It was a precision art with a definite set of rituals. The heist had to begin at an auspicious time: before sunrise. Dagad would set out between 4 and 5 a.m. when the road was still dark and meet with his associates at a predetermined location. It was a solemn start; the atmospherics had to be just right. As he prepared to leave, a code of silence was imposed on all other members of the household. If anyone interrupted that, it was a bad omen and the mission would have to be postponed to another, more auspicious day. At daybreak, Dagad would stand and smoke a beedi. Only when he was done could the operation begin. Each associate was told exactly where to go and what to do. The heists sometimes took three months, even six. And they always exposed Dagad to a world of travellers from distant lands. Big spenders from a class of people who were out of reach for him, except as a thief. It made Dagad resolve to change that for his children. Nothing would ever be out of reach for them. He would make sure of it. For his eight children, he wanted an English education and a different life.

It started with the small things, Dakxin explained. Even though his father almost never had enough money, he made sure Dakxin and his siblings lived in a world of dreams. It didn't weigh on him, for instance, that there was no electricity or tap water in Chharanagar. Or that women had to travel to a nearby lake to fill buckets of water and carry them back on their heads. Dakxin focused on an imaginary world. And on fantastic, unexplained phenomena, like the appearance of a TV set. TV was magic. But only one person had electricity and a TV in Chharanagar—the head of the panchayat or local council, Bachu Dada. So Dakxin and his friends landed up at his house every day just to stand outside and peer through the grill, and watch the magic box, transfixed. How did his favourite actors, like Amitabh Bachchan and Dharmendra, enter that little box? Or the radio for that matter? It was the biggest mystery in Dakxin's life until, one day, he found the answer. His father opened up their Murphy radio set to fix it. And out came a few knobbly parts. Eight little silver-and-blue cylindrical transistors. Dakxin saw them and concluded that these were mini-versions of his favourite actors. He ran to report this to his friends. 'The actors live inside the radio and TV,' he told his best friend Kalia, barely able to contain his excitement. 'They enter the box when no one is looking and then the bulb inside makes them expand and become really large. Then at night, when we're all asleep, they leave the box.'

There were a few rude interruptions in this fairy tale-like existence: the inescapable burden of being born a Chhara. It hit Dakxin one day when he was attending an English-medium school. There was a wedding nearby where the wealthy Sindhi community lived. That meant there would be an unmissably good spread of food laid out right under their noses. Dakxin's friends said that, since he was fair-skinned and could therefore pass off as Sindhi, he must scale the wall and steal some. He was nearly successful, hands full of golden-brown gulab jamuns, when his classmates, who were guests at the party, spotted him. 'There goes Dakxin the thief, the son of a thief!'

Another time, when he was ten years old and in class five, and his sister Koyna in class seven, she was paraded in front of the entire school during assembly as the girl who stole another kid's collection of marbles. It had to be her, the class teacher said to everyone, since she came from a family of thieves. Koyna's protestations of innocence were of no avail. Dakxin never forgot the look of humiliation in his sister's eyes. Their father thundered into the classroom the following day and beat up the teacher, but Koyna refused to go back to school. By then, Dakxin had also made up his mind that the English-medium school wasn't for him. He transferred to a Gujarati school.

But his father did not allow him to drop out. Dagad wanted his children to break the cycle of thievery; his perseverance paid off. Dakxin eventually got back to an English education, completing a master's in theatre and global development at the University of Leeds in the UK. He took a family legacy of acting skills needed for sleight of hand, and became a theatre actor and activist. And went on to make his first feature film, screened at theatres around the world.

Not all sons of thieves from Chharanagar had such glorious or heart-warming stories to tell. For Suresh, growing up was about the light going out of his eyes. There was no pride in being the son of a thief, no family history to be reiterated, no folklore to draw on. There was, in fact, no story. There were only ruptures and disaggregated pieces of his life that could later be used to describe the void.

It all came down to the father. While Dakxin's story was one of intimacy and belonging, Suresh's was about disease and defeat. As a child, Suresh contracted polio. The disease was rampant in India in the 1970s and an entire generation of 'polio kids' were marked by its side-effects—muscular dystrophy that sometimes stayed for life. Polio gave Suresh his middle name as a child, one everyone in Chharanagar used: Langdo, the limper. There was no getting away from it. His leg preceded him wherever he went—a visible, physical sign of failure. That's how his father Kanti Lal described it anyway.

Suresh was the oldest of five children. This, combined with the fact that he was a son, should have meant privilege. It should have earned him a place at the very top in the family hierarchy. Only, a freak of nature had caused it all to come apart for Suresh. To begin with, the father and mother wanted Suresh's bad leg to mend. So they followed what many in the area believed was the best form of healing. Bathing their son's leg in the blood of a pigeon. It had to be fresh to be effective. That meant catching and killing the bird and almost instantly extracting its blood. On one occasion, when

Kanti Lal went to trap a pigeon, he fell right through the wire-mesh into the well where the trap was laid. It caused the flesh to peel off his leg. He screamed in pain, cursed his son and gave up. 'He's going to remain like this, a one-legged limper. Good for nothing!'

The descriptor stuck and was implanted in Suresh's brain like a curse. Every time the kids in Chharanagar called him Langdo, it stung with the pain of being an unwanted child. Later, his classmates would describe him as the boy who was always angry. Afrezbhai Sheikh* saw this in him as he was growing up. He lived in Naroda Patiya—the Muslim neighbourhood adjoining Chharanagar—and went to school with Suresh. 'There were five or six of us who were always up to no good,' he recalled, smiling. 'We threw stones at the teacher and cursed like mad—motherfucker, sisterfucker,' he said and then quickly qualified: 'I was a bystander. I didn't use those words. Suresh and the others did.'

School in Chharanagar wasn't the best place to change hearts or minds. Bansidhar Acharya was a teacher in the area. He described how low the standards were when he started his career. People got a degree just for clearing class seven. 'It was called the Primary School Certificate and, on the basis of that, you could get a job as a primary school teacher.' To study any further, a parent would have to invest in bus transport for the child to travel out of the area to attend high school. While Dakxin's father did, Suresh's didn't. By the time he was in class two, Suresh and his gang were expelled from school for hitting a teacher on the head with a stone. He was expected to eventually take on the family trade of thieving. And he did.

'I've been seeing him since he was ten years old,' said a middle-aged man from the area. 'Suresh and my son got into a scuffle, he hit my son and stole his watch. I registered a complaint with the local police,' he said. 'And the cops came after Suresh and beat the crap out of him. They went on beating him, over and over,' the man said with a shudder. 'They beat him so much, even I felt bad. But then he is a Chhara after all. This is in their blood.'

Suresh did try and replace the moniker 'Langdo' with something positive, something he was crazy about—cricket. Despite his bad leg, he spent as much time as he could on the game, fashioning himself after his hero, who at the time was every cricket-crazy kid's idol. The West Indies team captain and one of the best batsmen ever to have played the game—Vivian Richards. When he was called 'Langdo', Suresh would yell back that everyone should call him Richard, only Richard. It seemed to have worked, at least in part. Suresh gradually took on the last name 'Richard'.

Over time, the police file on him put him down as Suresh 'Langdo' and Suresh Richard in equal measure. Over time, fewer and fewer people linked him with his father's last name, Suresh Kantibhai Jadeja. Over time, Suresh found his way out of the fractured family history through violence.

Abdul Majid had seen signs of it when Suresh was just sixteen years old—a quarter-century or more before 2002. At the corner of Chharanagar, where Majid sold crackly papad and other deep-fried snacks, Majid saw Suresh molest a girl. 'Because the Chharas were such big drinkers, my snacks lorry did very well in the area, so I made sure I was there every night, stocked with stuff to go with the booze,' he recalled. One evening, Suresh and his friend dragged a girl who was passing by into a by-lane, pinned her arms to her back and then whisked her away to the back of a workshop. She was screaming for help, but no one interfered. Majid decided that enough was enough, and stepped in. 'This is not at all okay. You cannot do this,' he said to the defiant teenager with angry black eyes. In return, Suresh got his friends to gang up and loot Majid's food cart.

The next day, Suresh's father met Majid, apologising profusely on his behalf. 'That sisterfucker bastard of a boy! He's not my son. I don't know whose son he is. I am really sorry, and I can't even pay you for the damages, I am not earning anything,' said Kantilal, who was more often than not to be found in a drunken stupor. And lost no opportunity to publicly shame his son. 'I don't know who that wife of mine has slept with to produce this bastard. He's not my blood. This boy is not my son,' Kantilal's voice would echo in the street.

FIVE

Dungar was an intelligent child. This was both a boon and a curse. It meant that he could not ignore the call of the jungle and all the possibilities of fun it offered, and quietly go to school instead. The thin forest cover near his village hadn't yet been destroyed by the onward march of progress and its prescriptive gobbling up of indigenous peoples' land to build highways. Peeking out from the layers of green were sleepy owls and noisy koyals, tiny flower-peckers, and fat brown buzzards with hooked beaks. Punctuating the patchwork forest and rolling hills were fields of corn. Shaky young stems, or stout, golden ripe ones. And towering over the corn fields and hills was a giant mango tree. It was so large that it took the arms of at least six children to embrace its trunk. Under its shade, on a hot summer morning, Dungar could bury himself in an underworld of yellow grasshoppers, red ladybirds, monstrous black beetles and half-eaten green mangoes. To replace such a sight with the four bland cement walls of a school was crazy. Cruel even. So Dungar skipped school as often as he could.

There was also a more prosaic reason to not go. His classmate Moti Sinh Baria* was the maker of very sharp blades. He waved them in Dungar's face every day and said to him, 'With these, I will cut you up. I'll cut you.' Moti wasn't from the Bhil clan like Dungar. He was upper caste, from the warrior Rajput lineage, which only added to Dungar's fear. So he left home each morning and spent the day under the mango or the mahuda tree. Since he was one of the brightest kids in class, his teacher wondered where he had disappeared to, and came around the house to inquire about him one sunny afternoon when Dungar was pretending to be at school.

'Why hasn't your boy been coming?' the teacher asked the nonplussed parents. 'But he's been going every day,' was their incredulous response. The next day, his father decided to follow Dungar in the morning. Just as the boy was squatting in his favourite spot, his father yanked him by the arm and said sternly, 'So this is where you've been?'

Dungar had nothing to say. He went to class the following day. But two days later, he skipped school again. This time, the teacher caught hold of him and beat him with a wooden baton. When he got home, his mother beat him. But Dungar was steadfast in his defiance. 'I will not go to school,' he declared. He had decided that he would rather suffer the beatings than be called out for his low social status by his classmates.

It wasn't as if school was a game changer either. Those who did finish ended up working in the fields as if they'd never studied at all. Some managed to get work as an electrician or a construction worker. That didn't give them more money or a better social status. But Dungar's grandparents had migrated from north Gujarat, where water was becoming scarce and farming impossible. They moved southward and eastward, and ended up as guards for upper-caste feudal barons. Education could potentially help make the transition to a government clerk or a police inspector, since the entrance exam required applicants to be graduates. Any government job was considered an elevated status for the Bhils and other tribals in the village. It gave them official authority and control to replace their fear of upper castes. That was perhaps why his parents and teacher pushed so hard.

The next time Dungar skipped school, they came down harder on him. They tied his hands and legs, and then beat him up. He managed to somehow undo the ropes and ran away to his uncle's house, stubbornness and self-will intact. After a couple of days, his father relented and said, 'Don't go to school, but come back home.' Dungar returned, had a bath and ate his meal in silence, only to have his father nag him again about going back to school. He ran away yet again and hid in the forest. But a cousin who had climbed a tall tree spotted him and declared to the family, 'I've found him! There he is!'

On the instructions of his teacher, Dungar was carried kicking and screaming to school by two boys. It was two in the afternoon and classes were over. He was taken to the empty classroom and a desk was brought down on his fingers. He had to stay that way for three hours. That day of excruciating pain was when things finally came to a head. 'Fine. I will go to school and stay in school and never come back home. Not even on a Sunday,' he declared to his parents. From then on, he started to live in his teacher's home, and do domestic chores for him in the afternoon in return for the boarding. It was the beginning of an altogether new phase in his life.

After a while, the teacher recommended to Dungar's parents that he stay in the school hostel. 'It will help him to study well and keep the right company,' he advised.

Dungar tried his best to find an agreeable set of kids to hang out with and focus on his studies. But he needed to start working, like many boys his age with no money for school fees or books. The only work readily available was at construction sites, a far cry from his life of a few months ago, spent flopped under a mahuda tree. He mostly got daily-wage jobs, breaking and lifting heavy stones or red sand. It was punishing, grinding work. As he lifted piles of bricks on his head, Dungar told himself that he had to find another way. This was not the life he wanted. It was not why he had left home. Sometimes, the drudgery and the physical exhaustion and, most of all, the low self-esteem made him wonder what it was all for.

'I was very angry and I also cried a lot,' Dungar said. 'I asked myself, why has this happened to me? Why do I have to do this?' And then a voice in his head, the stubborn part of him, pushed him forward: 'I must do this now so that I don't have to do it for the rest of my life.'

And things did seem to get better. His self-will was now buttressed by a tremendous force from the outside. That force was television and one programme in particular: Ramanand Sagar's *Ramayan*. Dungar came across it, completely by chance, on a trip he had made to a village nine kilometres away. It was the nodal area for the village council, or panchayat, to meet and, on most days, a busy, noisy place to be. But on the Sunday that Dungar went there, riding a friend's bicycle, the village was strangely silent. Everyone had gathered around the one TV at the panchayat office, as if it were some kind of oracle. On that screen, Dungar discovered the greatest show on earth. As golden horse-drawn chariots galloped in the air and the monkey god Hanuman turned into a giant, picking up the Himalayas in the palm of his hand, Dungar was transfixed.

His village had no electricity or TV. But now that he

knew that the serial was being telecast every Sunday at 9.30 a.m., Dungar had to find a way to get to the panchayat office to watch it. In 1987, Sunday mornings were *Ramayan* time across India. The country came to a grinding halt. Mothers stopped feeding their babies. Shopkeepers sent customers away. Politicians cancelled meetings. Now that Dungar had discovered this treasure, it became the single most important reason for him to live. From one Sunday to the next.

During the Diwali vacation, he went to stay with his elder sister, Susiben.* Her husband introduced Dungar to more specialised construction work—laying floor tiles—for which he was paid Rs 13 per day. One day, on the way to his sister's home, Dungar passed a bookstall at the local bus station. To his amazement, he saw a book that had a poster of *Ramayan* on its cover. He wanted it right away. He went up to the bookseller, a pleasant-looking Muslim man with a long beard and a stack full of bestsellers and religious books. 'How much is that one for?' he asked. '350 rupees,' was the reply. Dungar's heart sank. He only had 200 saved, but his mind was made up. He forced himself to do a few more back-breaking construction jobs to make the extra money. 'I bought that book,' Dungar remembered, his smile broadening and nostrils flaring. It was a moment of great pride.

For someone who had never read a book before, reading it through was a gruelling task. But the Ramayan was his new universe and he was consumed by it. After the day at school and work at a construction site, Dungar would cut back on his sleep so he could read. He kept a kerosene lamp by his bed and read a few pages before sleeping, then woke up at 4 a.m. each morning to read some more until 6. Paragraph by excruciating paragraph, he pushed himself. He had bought the book when he was in class 7. It took him till class 9 to finish it. In the process, he became an entirely self-taught reader. School, of course, wasn't a place where reading fluently was much of a focus.

'Reading the Ramayan made me feel really good,' Dungar said. 'The text had references to so many other books, like the Puran and the Mahabharat, so I started to buy those next,' he added. He bought himself a copy of the Mahabharat, then the Shiv Puran, the Garuda Puran, the Vishwakarma Puran. Construction jobs were taken on one after another with the singular purpose of saving up for the next book. In a village with a less than promising school education, it was in religion that Dungar found what he wanted most. A greater sense of self.

SIX

In the flat green plains of Pranav's village, religion was everywhere. During the nine-day Navratri festival, when the village was celebrating the divine feminine, a select group of people would declare that they were possessed by the spirit of the mother goddess. It was a phenomenon that captivated children and adults alike.

'They were regulars,' Pranav said, his usual mocking smile in place. The gyrating man and the woman with her hair hanging loose. These were the Navratras, when no one took chances with spirits. The nine days of fasting and feasting were meant to herald an auspicious new year. Everyone prayed for a bumper crop of wheat since it was nearly harvest time in a village that, despite a few hundred tubewells, depended quite substantially on the rain. Even the sceptics, of whom there were many, didn't want to upset the performers—just in case the mother goddess really was watching. Pranav and his gang of friends decided they would play sleuths and catch those faking the spirit-possession.

'We noticed that the ground in front of these people was uneven,' Pranav explained. 'There was a deep pit right in front, but they never fell in.' If they were aware enough to mind their step, could they really be inhabited by ghosts? There was another dead giveaway—the transformation of their voices. When a crowd appeared, they sounded ominous and otherworldly. When there was no audience around, their voices slipped back to normal. Pranav and his friends were inclined to conclude they were fakes. Only one thing held them back. 'We didn't dare challenge them for fear of being slapped for our impertinence,' Pranav explained.

The possibility of impertinence, though, was only one of many caste-endowed privileges that Pranav enjoyed, even if his family had very little money. His father was a tubewell operator. They lived modestly, and had a two-acre plot of land that provided enough wheat for subsistence, none for making a profit. By the time Pranav was a school-going part-time investigator of spirit-possessed villagers, the water table in the area had started to drop. Tubewells went dry. Their small plot gave less and less produce over time. Pranav's father, though, was a people-magnet. Nothing in his circumstance suggested power, not his meagre resources, nor his unglamorous job. It did not have to. His position came from a place beyond these considerations, a religion-sanctioned hierarchy. And it meant that the liveliest, most irreverent conversation could be conducted in the courtyard outside their home. Usually over endless rounds of card games. Especially kannastar, the Indian version of rummy, minus the betting and money.

In Pranav's village, like in most of India, hierarchy dictated geography. Houses were stratified to maintain caste purity. Their house was in a section with the widest street. It was flanked by a large cattle enclosure on one side. Every enclave had its own tubewells and cattle, so no one consumed milk or drank water from spaces occupied by lower castes. In contrast with the concrete homes on Pranav's street, with their mosaic-tiled courtyards in orange, pink, blue and green, were the mud-and-thatch homes at the other end. These were the homes of the Dalits. The people who cleared garbage and picked up the carcasses of dead cows to sell to tanneries. Pushed to the farthest extremity of the village, out of sight.

There was also a large Muslim enclave in the village with a population that was nearly as large as the caste Pranav came from. Two generations ago, they were wealthy merchants along a busy trade route. Over time, their money and status were eroded by the churn caused by Partition and the rise of other powerful caste groups. Some now lived in mid-sized homes with large courtyards. Others had more modest accommodations built of mud walls and thatched roofs. Whether middling or poor, no Muslim home in this village had goats tethered to the front porch, as they might elsewhere in Gujarat. Such was their fear of the Hindu, vegetarian, powerful landed castes in whose fields most Muslims earned daily wages. They did not want to cause offence by slaughtering goats or cooking meat.

It was important for the geographical separation to be maintained silently and effectively. Everything counted—from the location of the house to the well people drew water from. There had to be a balance between being at ease and looking over one's shoulder to see who was creeping up behind. Pranav learned this through osmosis and observation. The front porch, where his father was the arbiter of many lively discussions between believers and the minority group of dissenting atheists, was one kind of theatre for such schooling.

'Give me a stick so I can go break all the idols,' he once heard a guest say. 'Oh my god, how can you speak like this!' another reacted. The power to accommodate dissent—that was what Pranav's father and friends had in their grasp. It was his first exposure to the possibility that beliefs could be questioned. But this dexterity depended on a careful balance. That was the subtext. The more unusual conversations were buried in a sea of other, more commonplace ones. On the way things were meant to be and the minor irritants that the people on the other side of the village posed with their strange habits. The azaan in their mosques that disturbed the calm, especially during exam season. It was cathartic to express the irritation by repeating the common refrain, 'These Muslims should be taught a lesson.'

Pranav's fairly unremarkable young life was sent into an exciting spin when he joined the local boy scouts. It was the promise of adventure that made him sign up. In the beginning, there were mini military drills and march pasts. 'Stand at ease, attention! Forward maaaaarch ... lef–ri–lef–lef–lef.' It was all about drumming some discipline into the bodies and minds of these youngsters. Only, for Pranav, it was an opportunity to do the exact opposite—to be undisciplined—that was attractive. The real reason he had enlisted was because all the boy scouts would be taken out of town for boot camp. Out of the sight of their parents and strictly imposed codes of behaviour.

The first trip out, when Pranav was in class six, came with an inbuilt challenge. The teacher accompanying the group was known to his parents, which made things harder. But Pranav had his mind made up. Nothing would get in the way of using this trip as a break-out moment. 'The only thing we had to worry about was our supervisor. If he found out, then bas ... finished!' Pranav said. He and his friends had figured out what sin they wanted to commit. The abomination of eating eggs. The one thing that was strictly forbidden in their homes. Eating eggs and meat was tantamount to defiling their purity, so it was especially exciting. 'We had never eaten eggs, so we said ki, haan, at least once we must try it,' Pranav recounted, his eyes gleaming.

In the Gujarat of the 1980s, eggs were like drugs. They were sold openly in tiny grocery stores owned and run by Muslims, Christians, Parsis or lower-caste Hindus. In neighbourhoods like Pranav's, there was no question of buying them in shops and taking them back home. Eggs were sold cooked—on the street, and in food stalls frequented by boys from 'decent' homes in secret, when their parents and the friends of parents weren't looking. Boiled-egg lorries and masala-omelette carts were parked in mixed residential zones, or just outside the area where the nice people lived. After dark, under the light of brightly shining bulbs, boiled eggs with their yellow yolks evoked temptation in the young and unspoiled. The sprinkle of tangy rock salt on top took away the strangeness of the smell, making the pieces cut in four curved quarters even more inviting.

At the scouts' camp, Pranav and his friends had spotted an egg lorry on the way to their morning training. They made an elaborate plan to get to it after dark, away from the prying eyes of the supervising teacher from their village. There was an added impediment. The teacher had a young nephew who was in class seven and part of the camp. There was only one way out. To include the nephew in the insurrection. If he snitched, he would be telling on himself as well. Fortunately for them, the teachers were housed in a separate building. Pranav and his friends were patient. They waited until after dinner to scale the wall behind their compound.

It was pitch dark and they had made it past the wall when the teacher's nephew suddenly panicked. 'I'm going to head back, I'm feeling scared,' he declared to the rest. 'There's fifteen of us here with you, what's there to be scared of?' Pranav had asked, trying his best to pacify him. Eventually, he had to be sent back with the warning that if he squealed on them, they would tell everyone he was part of it. With the last obstacle cleared, it was time to eat.

They pooled their day's pocket money and bought the eggs. Each egg was cut into neat little quarters and four scouts shared one. They drowned the eggs in a ton of masala and gulped down their respective pieces. 'It tasted just about okay. But that didn't matter,' Pranav said. 'It felt good.' This is what it took to grow up: crossing a threshold of fear. No one at home needed to know. Conversations with parents were to be kept to a bare minimum.

'There was this thing about me,' Pranav explained. 'I never spoke much. And I would never say ki now I am going out to play cricket, now I am going here, now I am going there. What was the point of saying so much? I was home when I was required to be, so what was the big deal?' This always upset his parents, who constantly contrasted Pranav's unwillingness to communicate with his younger brother who reported every move at all times. 'Until I was in class seven, we did not have a toilet at home. We had to go to a place near the local pond with an Amul ghee ka dabba or a plastic bottle or something,' Pranav said, grinning. 'It used to be great fun. We'd set out in a gang and hang out together for hours after, playing cricket. And when we got back, my parents would remark that I had taken three hours to do something that takes ten minutes. From then only I had decided that it's pointless to account for my activities. I will just listen to what they have to say, and speak when spoken to.'

For being deferential when required, Pranav's parents allowed him the occasional indulgence. He could skip a family ritual or two, such as fasting during the Navratri celebration, if he asked nicely. Having grown into an egg-eating, rule-defying youngster, Pranav was beginning to demonstrate signs of rebellion in other areas of his life too, and it could not stay hidden from his parents. He had no desire to study science, as his father had expected him to. Pranav knew well before he got to class ten that, when the time came to choose what he wanted to study after, he would pick the arts stream. He knew also that the natural order of things dictated the opposite. Certain that no real jobs could be had after an arts degree, his father just assumed that Pranav would pick science like all the other boys.

The class ten board exam hung like a dark shadow over his head. It was going to be very hard to have an adult conversation with his father about this. Fathers were meant to be revered and feared a little, and his own had a temper. Pranav had never been at the receiving end of a tirade, but he had seen his younger brother being hit for mimicking their father's swagger while smoking cigarettes. Pranav had side-stepped most confrontations by spending his days outdoors. Circumstance, too, had played its part. The school in the village only went up to class seven, after which Pranav had been sent out to a private school in the big town nearby. He was given a monthly allowance and his own bicycle, and that meant a certain amount of independence. But the freedom came at a price. He was meant to deliver what was expected.

His very first open rebellion was brutally crushed. Father would have none of it: science it had to be. Pranav, not strong enough then to stand his ground, gave in. But the discontent simmered, eventually snowballing into a full-fledged revolt two years later. His time of reckoning was the big board exam at the end of class twelve, which would determine the kind of college he could get into after, and therefore set the path for his career. It was payback time. He failed in two subjects out of five. Physics and Maths. It was a major embarrassment for his parents, and an inconvenient truth stared them in the face. That they no longer had a hold over their son.

'My parents had huge expectations. They wanted me to do a BSc after class twelve, but my mind was in some other place. I knew I was going to fail. In Physics especially, I was a hundred per cent sure of failing. Even my friends knew I couldn't pass. I never used to attend classes only! In fact, I thought that if I passed, I would have a much bigger problem to deal with. If I just got rid of science, it would be a big relief, and for that I was willing to do anything,' Pranav explained.

His father was so angry after the results that he refused to communicate directly with Pranav. He spoke instead to the boy's friends, 'Go talk to him and ask him what he wants to do.' The friends tried to play the placatory role they had been assigned, but Pranav was unrepentant and determined. He knew that giving in at this stage and agreeing to pore over science for another year would only set him up for more failure. This time around, he stuck to his guns and insisted that he would pursue the arts stream. 'Do whatever you like then,' was his father's steely reply.

After this flashpoint, as is often the case, both sides were in an altered state. Pranav established his independence. His parents no longer pinned any hopes on their son. They wrote him off as a drifter who had no idea what he wanted to do beyond playing cricket with his friends.

Now that he had struck out against his parents and chosen the arts, there was a trade-off. His mother set him up for some remedial classes in the summer. Spiritual training to improve the mind. These were classes in Hinduism and meditation conducted by women who had chosen to be celibate and dedicate themselves to god. They were called

Brahma Kumaris, and had started out, ironically enough, as a group of rebellious women. The singular spiritual pursuit had been an escape from forced arranged marriages. It allowed them to declare to the world that they were married to god and, therefore, unavailable to men.

In the 1930s, this was a subversive phenomenon. But by the 1980s, it had been mainstreamed and thousands of women across the country flocked to it, and the Brahma Kumaris were anything but rebellious. They were called upon by Pranav's mother with the express purpose of taking the fight out of him. She summoned her son and told him flatly, 'Since you've failed your exams, I am asking you to spend one hour of your day doing something good.' Pranav was out of manoeuvres and reluctantly agreed to what was supposed to be a spiritual overhaul. He made just one request, for the lectures to be held in their home. He didn't want to be the object of ridicule amongst his friends for attending sermons that were generally seen as the pursuit of geriatrics.

Luckily for him, this fitted in with the Brahma Kumaris' own plans. They were looking for a place to host their sermons. The talks began in Pranav's home, with a group of regulars sitting in. The average age of the group was around sixty; Pranav was eighteen. He attended the sermons for six months, but his restive mind could not bear it for much longer. So Pranav slowly but surely plotted an exit for himself.

In Pranav's home, the Brahma Kumari, dressed in a pristine white sari, was seated on a chair. The rest of the gathering sat on the ground in front of her, cross-legged, backs straight, eyes closed. A guided meditation followed. Voices dropped to the familiar low hum. 'Ohm. Ohhhhhhhhhhm.' Inhale. Exhale. All eyes on the preacher as she began a discussion on the Hindu cycle of birth, death and rebirth. After the talk, Pranav approached her.

'You say we are all part of a cosmic cycle and each soul has eighty-four lives, is that correct?' he asked.

'Yes, that's correct,' was the reply.

'You also said that each soul has a point of reckoning in this karmic cycle with Lord Shiva and that it's all preordained by him, isn't it?'

The Brahma Kumari nodded in agreement.

And then Pranav hit her with his carefully planned barb. 'Well, if everything is pre-decided by god, then what difference does it make whether I pray or not?'

Everything that was said after this moment was a blur. All that Pranav was certain of was that, from then on, he was let off the hook altogether. Excused from attending any more sermons.

SEVEN

In Chharanagar, stories about Suresh were becoming legend. Hanifbhai,* an auto-rickshaw driver who grew up with him, had a story to tell. Hanif was waiting for customers at the Chharanagar–Naroda Patiya intersection. It was a Sunday, just a little before dark. Street vendors had begun to re-fry semi-cooked chicken lollies in rancid oil; the air was filled with a stale smell. Suddenly, a young woman ran in the direction of Hanif and his friends.

'Please, Bhai—' she started to say, completely out of breath.

Just then, a man caught up with her and interjected, 'Don't let her out of your sight. Make sure she's standing right here, I am just coming back.'

Hanifbhai recognised him as a friend of Suresh's. 'Why, what's the matter, Bhai?' he inquired.

The question was met with an impatient repetition of the original instruction. 'You just make sure she stays right here. I'll be back in two minutes,' the man said and disappeared into the evening dust.

As soon as he was gone, the young girl turned to them and said, 'Can I tell you something?' She sounded hesitant. 'All of you—you can do what you like with me. But please, I beg you, take me back to my home,' she pleaded with the startled group. 'These people have kept me with them forcibly for the last three days and they've been taking turns to rape me,' the girl said plaintively.

Hanif and his friends had to make a quick mental calculation before they replied. Suresh was a young adult by now, and one whom everyone feared and kept away from. 'Why don't you just make a dash for it and run? We'll support you in that. We'll say we failed to stop you,' Hanif said. 'But we can't take you home.'

'No, no!' the girl cried out. 'If I try and run, they'll hunt me down. Please just take me home,' she pleaded.

Such was their fear of Suresh that Hanifbhai and his friends decided it was a risk they could not take. By this time, the man who had deposited the girl was back and Suresh was right beside him. The girl froze where she stood. So did Hanif. And then Suresh and his friends dragged her away, pinned her down on a bike and disappeared into the snake-like gullies of Chharanagar. Hanifbhai never found out what happened to her.

Tales of bestiality attached themselves to Suresh, feeding the city's voyeurism. In actual fact, there were similar acts committed and often overlooked by people in other parts of Chharanagar. There was the story, for instance, that Guddu, who also lived in Chharanagar, narrated. It was a fable from his childhood, about the woman who came to pick up the garbage. 'People would try and touch her private parts. And then she ran away.'

Another story: Guddu was attending a wedding along with his fiancée and her parents, and made it a point to strike up a conversation with his father-in-law-to-be. As they filled their dinner plates, he saw a woman headed in their direction. She bent down and touched the father-in-law's feet. 'This is my brother's wife, your aunt-in-law-to-be,' the older man informed Guddu. But as soon as she was out of sight, he turned around and bragged, 'And I've fucked her about twenty-five times.' The sordid details were rolled out next. 'She calls me once her husband is away at work. I enter her room and take off her clothes.' Guddu choked on his food, unable to digest this talk. Later, he put the unprocessed matter into a safe box on which he stuck a label that many in Chharanagar used to describe similar phenomenon—'those filthy people from the other side'.

There were, in effect, two Chharanagars. The one where Guddu's father-in-law and Suresh came from—Chhota Chharanagar, or Lesser Chharanagar. Also known as Manjhnyavas. 'Those people talk in a foul way all the time. That is how they are,' Guddu said, looking back on his broken engagement. In that part of the sprawling shanty, the streets were narrower and the houses bunched up against each other.

Right beside it was the Chharanagar where Guddu came from. It was called Bada Chharanagar, or Kubernagar. Some of the houses here were two-storeyed and had terraces. A few metres down the main street was the Kubernagar railway crossing. Across it, the road led to a house with bright green ivy wrapped around the front porch. This was the façade of a one-room library. It was an unusual sight in the middle of Bada Chharanagar, and was singularly responsible for injecting an entirely different kind of influence into its surroundings. The library was the meeting ground for the Budhan Theatre group, which was set up in the 1990s. A world away from the den Suresh lived in.

It was home to drama and poetry and the new ideas planted there by two revolutionaries. The Bengali writer and champion of tribal rights, Mahasweta Devi. And the linguist and tribal rights activist, Professor Ganesh Devy. Together, they set up the Budhan library and theatre group that gave people like Dakxin Chhara a completely different way of seeing. The exposure Dakxin had through Budhan revealed to him a world-changing truth close to home: the history of the oppression of his people. It allowed him to not be ashamed of being tribal and, therefore, not be sucked into propaganda that feasted on low self-esteem. It made Dakxin proud of his ancestry.

One street away from Suresh, this was a completely different world.

No one knew why the two roads to Chharanagar had diverged, or when. Why Chhota Chharanagar was considerably poorer and more decrepit than Bada. Why it was that neither Suresh nor anyone from his street crossed over to the other side to join Budhan. But when stories of violence and rape were told, the residents of Bada Chharanagar would shrug, roll their eyes and declare, 'That is not us. It's them. We hardly know them.'

In Bada Chharanagar, Dakxin grew up entirely unaware of any polarisation between the Chharas and the Muslims. In Chhota Chharanagar, on the other hand, the growing rift between the two communities was impossible to ignore. The Muslim hamlet of Naroda Patiya was just one street away. Chhota Chharanagar and Patiya were twin ghettos where Muslims and Chharas worked side by side and in competition with each other. Both communities were butchers and meat vendors. At a time when the rest of the country was experiencing a new wave of Hindu evangelism in the 1990s, Chhota Chharanagar became the perfect swamp for animosity to fester. It was in this part of Ahmedabad city, which the law and justice systems had long ignored, that the most testosterone-driven, sabre-rattling arm of the Hindu right—the Bajrang Dal—decided to proselytise. People with saffron bands and sharp three-pronged tridents had begun to organise weekend camps close to Chharanagar, and these were eventually attended by Suresh and many like him.

In the year 1992, the Bajrang Dal asked its members to carry out a special mission that they said would herald a new golden age of Hindu rule. At meetings, their leaders conjured up an image of a dark and terrible present. This was an age of misrule, members were told. The ruling Congress party only catered to the heathens—the Muslims—to stay in power. This was the highest form of disrespect to the Hindus and to the god Ram. Leaders spoke of what an abomination it was that, in the city of Ayodhya in Uttar Pradesh, on the exact spot where Ram was born, stood a sixteenth-century mosque. How it was built by an evil Muslim ruler and how the present government spent its time appeasing his descendants. Muslims were a threat to the idea of resurrecting a new golden age of Hindus. Down with the Babri masjid, the mosque built by Babur. Down with Muslims, children of Babur. Armies of Hindus now had a task at hand. To go to Ayodhya and bring down the mosque. And build a Ram temple in its place.

The Ayodhya campaign was designed to dazzle. It was a clever fusion of religion, historical fiction and middle-class aspiration, designed by the Hindu-majoritarian BJP's most popular leader, L.K. Advani. He was aided in this task by a rising star in the party: Narendra Modi. They knew that there was a restless and untapped middle class to be enticed and that aspirational people needed a platform to look good. And the Advani–Modi duo delivered. They called their nationwide campaign a Rath Yatra, a chariot ride, like that of Hindu gods. Except that the actual beast was the very non-mythic and aspirational Toyota bus, fitted with air-conditioning and broadcast facilities. Suddenly, god-like scenes from the *Ramayan* television series had come alive. Thousands of Hindus heard this clarion call. And on 6 December 1992, they brought the Babri masjid down.

Suresh didn't go to Ayodhya like many others from Gujarat. But he was caught up in the tidal wave of Hindu evangelism that went with it and all the accompanying propaganda against Muslims. Hanifbhai said that he now detected a distinct difference in Suresh's behaviour. Before the demolition, he hung out quite unselfconsciously with his Muslim friends.

He did have Muslim friends. If people like Abdul Majid and Hanifbhai had been fearful enough of Suresh to not get in the way of his molesting women, then why would they hang around with him for chai and beedis at all? Hanifbhai said it was to counter other powerful dons from their own community. In the ghetto of Naroda Patiya, across the street from Chharanagar, there were Muslim equivalents of Suresh. It was a neighbourhood outside the pale of the law, just like Chharanagar was. It had its own strongmen with 'protectorates' carved out. If a local from Naroda Patiya was in trouble with one of these strongmen, or owed one of their protectees money, then they had to cultivate another strongman to save themselves. This was where Suresh stepped in. His sphere of influence extended from Chharanagar to a few friends in Naroda Patiya.

'He could deal with the bhais, the dons in our area. So people in our area cultivated him specifically for that reason,' Hanif explained. In fact, Hanifbhai had even joined the Bajrang Dal because Suresh was in it. Over a session of chai and beedis, Suresh had told him about this new group and suggested that he come along as well, not knowing at the time what the Dal was about. They even went to a few meetings together.

It was only later, after the demolition of the Babri mosque, that Hanif asked him what the Bajrang Dal was really about. Suresh had replied, 'Hanifbhai, you should just leave.' Hanif quit the Dal. He also noticed that Suresh's anger was increasingly directed at Muslims. He stole their goats. And even stole from twelve-year-old children. A group of Muslim boys was coming back home on a Saturday, pockets jingling with the week's wages from working at a tailoring unit in the area. Suresh waylaid them and made off with their money. By now, Hanifbhai's chai sessions with Suresh had come to a stop. Instead of calling Hanifbhai by his name, Suresh had begun to use 'miya'—the pejorative for Muslims. 'Chal, Miya, get out of here,' he said.

In the middle of this zealous indoctrination, Suresh discovered to his horror that his sister had eloped with a Muslim man. She had changed her name from Sita to Shamim. The humiliation Suresh felt was more than he could handle. His sister had anticipated this when she fell in love with an auto-rickshaw driver called Nasir Khan Pathan. Her fear of Suresh was so great that Nasir and she had run away to the coastal town of Khambat, ninety kilometres from Ahmedabad. They should have known that he was unstoppable. Suresh went after her to Khambat, expecting to succeed in bringing Sita back. She not only refused to return but also threatened to call the police. His rage was now completely out of control. It found an outlet when his sister least suspected it.

A year and a half went by, and Sita suggested to Nasir that they make a trip back home to reconnect with her family and try and patch things up with Suresh. She had two sons from her previous marriage whom she had left behind, and was unable to meet for fear of her brother's wrath. They made a trip back, and Nasir sent word to Suresh that they should meet and talk. Suresh agreed. They sat across each other in a chai shop and had an amicable conversation. 'The next day,' Nasir said, his voice quivering as he narrated the story, 'I was sitting on the same bench at the same dhaba when I was suddenly attacked from behind by thirteen men.'

Nasir was a tiny man. His sunken eyes, yellow possibly from the constant consumption of intoxicants, turned away as he spoke. Suresh's men had swung a chain around Nasir from behind, catching him unawares. They tied him to a chair, shoved him into an auto-rickshaw and drove him to an empty lot at the back of Chharanagar. They pulled him out of the auto and hit him with iron pipes. They broke several bones—both hands were smashed—before they abandoned him there.

Nasir and Sita ran back to Khambat and severed all ties with the family. Sita, who looked like a plumper version of Suresh—stout, with sharp black eyes and hair dyed maroon with mehendi—said she would never talk about that time or her family again.

In Chharanagar, Suresh talked about it a lot. To all and sundry, he declared, 'They have taken one of mine, I will take one of theirs.' He set himself a task to appease his rage: finding a Muslim wife.

ॐ

It may appear at this juncture in the story that Suresh's life was moving inexorably towards 28 February 2002, and all that the day held. But that is merely the distortion caused by telling this story backwards. Hindsight that prevents us from looking carefully at other potential Sureshs growing up in Chharanagar. Why him and not his two brothers, for instance? Similar acts of savagery are rumoured to have been associated with at least one of them. But they are nowhere in the picture of 2002. And there is also the question of the way in which people like Suresh, Dungar and, to some extent, Pranav are often written about. As instruments in the hands of the machinery of the Hindu right. As if this was a one-way process, and the instruments did nothing to shape the machine. And as if everything that was said was taken on as is, unprocessed. As if the planners amongst the upper castes and wealthy communities planned it all and the mob just followed orders.

It draws attention to how each of the three actors here were not marionettes, being pulled by a dark gravitational force over which they had no control. Neither were they operating on a blank canvas over which they had absolute creative rights.

For every Suresh Langdo, there were many more Dakxins and Guddus in Chharanagar. And that there were goondas in the Muslim ghetto of Naroda Patiya gets glossed over only because that is where people were massacred. And that brings us to the very complicated question of birth and circumstance. What part of his ancestry did Pranav hold on to, or Dungar for that matter?

EIGHT

On most mornings, while Dungar was getting used to a new life in his schoolteacher's home, his father was lying around inebriated in a neglected field. 'He used to drink a lot,' Dungar recalled, frowning. 'And then he would lose his temper and beat my mother up. That made me feel terrible. I decided it was good that I wasn't living at home.' Dungar had begun to feel a rising anger towards his father. This was wholly unremarkable, except that it got mixed up with the humiliation he had faced in his early years for being Bhil. Now that he was living in his teacher's house, there was a readily available role model to provide contrast. His teacher was upper caste, Hindu, God-fearing and vegetarian. And he did not touch alcohol. So Dungar began to process his father's drinking problem as something that was intrinsic to being Bhil. Being tribal. His adolescent mind took his personal history and tied it to the notion that he came from a failed society. There was about him a shiftiness of gaze, a hunching of the shoulders, a polite smile that drooped slightly awkwardly at the edges. And a permanent desire to be someone else—his guru. Everything his father was not. Everything a Bhil was not.

Dungar decided to copy his teacher's lifestyle entirely. 'I used to stay with Guruji. He would wake up early and start his day with a puja and the lighting of incense sticks. So I also started doing that,' Dungar said. It was the small things that made all the difference. Standing still next to his guru and watering the plants. Watching the morning dew form cool glassy beads on the tulsi leaves. Pearls in transit. In the blink of an eye, they were gone. One day, Dungar's mentor took him to a sermon that was another watershed moment. It was a spiritual discourse by Gujarat's most widely regarded guru of the time—Morari Bapu. He was always dressed in white, with a trademark black tilak on his forehead. And he was famous for telling stories from the Ramayan as popular folklore.

'The Ramcharitmanas is not just a book,' Morari Bapu would often say. 'It is the very heart of the sages of this country.' As he sat in his white vest, his friendly white beard catching a glint of sun, the god-man described a world that was unpredictable and mind-expanding. For instance, he said that the most illuminating character in the Ramayan was not the lord himself but a character who supposedly represented evil. The sister of the demonic Ravan. The dark and desire-filled woman Shurpanakha, who lusted after Ram's brother and was spurned by him. It was she who set the Ramayan on its epic course of revenge, Morari Bapu explained. And like an ace storyteller, he would always give Dungar's favourite story a completely fresh spin.

'The universe is made up of two kinds of people—those who are attached to the world and those who are detached from it. Pravrutti and Nivrutti,' he said in one of his sermons. 'If you look at the brother of Bhagvan Ram, you will see how he represents detachment. Think about it,' Bapu urged. 'He left his home to follow Ram, he left his parents, his wife, his children.' Bapu paused for effect before getting to the heart of the matter. 'Surpanakha, on the other hand, lived in Lanka. The fiery place. She represents attachment, desire, an active force.' He paused again and then drove his point home: 'In the extreme, neither attachment nor detachment are good. Ram and Sita represent that mid-point, that balance of forces between the two. That, my friends, is what we need in our lives.'

It was impossible not to lean in to the stories Morari Bapu told. They were layered and complex, and yet it all felt so accessible and applicable to the present. 'It was winter. It was cold and there were lots of people at Bapu's sermons,' Dungar remembered. 'We sat for three-hour sessions for three consecutive days. And I was inspired. Truly. It made me believe that there was really a god. It felt like I was in a divine presence. One that I must be in touch with every day by praying alongside my guru.'

Morari Bapu's sermons had shown the lonely young Dungar a new world. Its power surged through him as he began to consume religious sermons voraciously and sing bhajans better than everyone else. 'I sang so well that everyone would remark—just look at that boy! We must call Dungar to sing at the next session.' For the first time in his life, he was being noticed. It felt fantastic. So Dungar took it a step further and organised the Navaratri celebration in his village. Even though this was the biggest festival in Gujarat, the village didn't have a celebration of their own. Now that Dungar was organising it in the school premises, everyone was excited about the tak-tchik-tak of sticks beating to the Garba dance, the girls in their backless blouses and mirror-work cholis.

It was a slow and steady transition for Dungar until a terrible event speeded it up. On 31 October 1984, the prime minister of India, Indira Gandhi, was assassinated. The announcement was made late in the evening on All India Radio. Dungar saw how everyone in the village was speaking about it in hushed tones for fear of not knowing which way the wind would blow next. His family, like most people in Gujarat, had voted for Mrs Gandhi's party, the Congress, but her death caused a political earthquake. It gave the BJP the perfect opportunity to step in and build on a growing resentment of her. The political complexion of Gujarat was reversed in the next decade, and Dungar was an integral part of that change.

Leaders in the BJP noticed the exuberance with which Dungar participated in and organised religious programmes. It would be a few years before they officially started their campaign to build a Ram temple at Ayodhya. But they already had a vision for combining religion with politics: to create an idea of a greater Hindu state by appealing to a new aspirational class. They were observing Dungar and others like him carefully. From 1985 onwards, the local leader enlisted him as a volunteer to campaign in an election. He was only twelve years old and in class seven, but Dungar sensed that this was an appetiser before the main course. It made him feel important to go from door to door and shout alongside party campaigners, 'If you are a true Hindu, there is only one party for you. The BJP.'

He had also begun to attend meetings organised by the BJP's religious affiliates, the VHP and the Bajrang Dal. It was like time travel. Those who attended felt like modern-day incarnations of Lord Ram's army—troopers led by the monkey-god Hanuman. It was almost like living inside his favourite TV serial. Dungar imagined he was part of a new spiritual churn that would recreate the age of Ram. A new wave of militant, trishul-wielding tribal youth had signed up in the thousands to defend the faith. Bajrangi gyms started to pop up in the local town with posters of beefed-up bodies.

This new identity felt bigger and better than the shaky one he had grown up with. Even though the tribal population in his village was large, the numbers did not reduce their feeling of inadequacy. The words Bhil, adivasi and tribal were used by all the other castes, whether upper or backward, as pejoratives. It was telling that Dungar's family history changed with each successive recounting in an attempt to create a non-tribal past to elevate his present.

'We are Rajputs,' Dungar would insist, claiming an upper-caste warrior lineage for himself. Even though their present was entirely Bhil. His father had seven wives, which wasn't uncommon amongst those of the tribe. His family spoke a local dialect of Bhili. On the evening of Diwali, Dungar's father would call a shaman to perform a trance-like ritual and invoke the mother-goddess Kali. Clay diyas would be lit with wicks dipped in the local toddy. Clay horses crafted by the tribe would be placed beside them as objects of worship. The shaman would shake and writhe on the floor after consuming the toddy, and declare to the worshippers that the mother goddess was now present in his body. They could place their demands before 'her'. Then the ritual would be over and the shaman would lie limp in a post-trance state, and the group would drink and dance in a communal stupor. A chicken or a goat would be beheaded, cooked and consumed to round off the festivities. Dungar insisted that, even though his father performed all the required tribal rituals, he was actually upper caste and used a last name that was half Bhil and half Rajput.

'I bribed my way into my tribalness,' Dungar declared proudly to anyone he needed to convince about having a worthier lineage. 'I know what it took for me to buy my scheduled tribe certification. I bribed an officer in 1992 with 5,000 rupees,' he said. 'We are not really tribal, you know. When I was in the seventh standard, my grandfather was alive and I asked him what community we really come from. He said we were Thakurs [a word often used to describe Rajputs]. When he migrated from the north to where we live now, he mingled with the tribals, since the area is mostly populated by them. He took a tribal girl for himself and was excommunicated from his caste. Since my grandfather was tossed out of his caste group, my father and the next generation adopted a tribal life. My father changed the caste name from Thakur. He still beheads a chicken on festivals, like the other Bhils do, but we are not truly tribal.'

To dispel any doubt, he explained further, 'Hardly anyone in this area is genuinely from one of the tribes or castes in the scheduled list. They've all bribed their way in to avail of government reservations for jobs and education. Everyone is adulterated.'

The new identity Dungar was forging for himself made him an even better target for the Hindu right. This low self-esteem is what allowed the Sangh Parivar to draw him so easily into its fold as a forever-insecure Hindu. Someone who needed to first be told what he did not have, so that he would always be dependent on handouts from its leaders for self-improvement. An entire culture was crafted around the idea of becoming a bhagat—a person who gave up alcohol and meat. This made sense to Dungar in other ways as well. It helped ease the pain he grew up with, the tears he had to fight as a boy watching his alcoholic father beat his mother up. If alcohol was essential to the Bhil way of life, and had turned out to be such a shattering experience, he was happy to do away with both.

To compound Dungar's anxiety about his identity was the fact that, in the 1980s, when he was growing up, it put him at the bottom of the social hierarchy, lower even than the Muslims of the area. To be placed by the Sangh at the very bottom of the Hindu hierarchy was one thing. To be lower than those considered to be heathens was too much to bear. Muslims were mostly traders and much wealthier than people like him. Their houses were bigger and better, and they had no trouble asserting their supremacy. At a streetside chicken biryani shop, six kilometres from Dungar's village, a group of Muslim men spoke of how it used to be. 'They turned up in torn clothes or just underpants. They had no footwear. Their feet were caked with mud. They were generally dirty. So, on their own, they never sat at the same level as us. And we never let them either.'

While Muslims spoke clearly identifiable languages—Urdu and Gujarati—with lineages of power and history attached, Dungar was embarrassed to acknowledge the existence of the tribal language in which he often spoke with his parents. 'Our language is quite crude,' Dungar said quietly. 'It's a language with no name.' He was unaware of an entire branch of study that painstakingly sought to preserve his language with its name. Back then, in any case, that discovery wasn't accessible to him. So he grabbed his new-found pride in being Hindu with both hands, and made what he could of it. He did sometimes admit that he didn't know if that was where he truly belonged either.

The confusion stemmed from the fact that tribals were not, historically speaking, Hindus at all. They had a complex history of moving in and out of the Hindu fold. This reality, however, was too far removed from Dungar's life. Only much later, and very gradually, would he become aware that tribals elsewhere, in other villages in Gujarat, were in a similar predicament: should they or should they not accept the offerings of the Sangh.

It was hard to erase everything from his past, though. Especially since his childhood had so many happy moments. Perhaps it was possible to pretend, while actually conceding nothing. 'It was mostly for show,' Dungar said of the Hinduisation he had undergone. Becoming vegetarian and non-drinking in a village of drinkers—'It helped change your status,' he said. Dungar was painfully aware of the fact that he was nothing without status. One brush with the police was always enough to show people their place. Fear was an abominable thing, and a constant when you are at the bottom of the social hierarchy. It's why his grandfather had become a guard. It was why most Bhils wanted some sort of state power at their disposal. So that it would not be continually used against them.

'In those days, there was no proper road to our village, so we had very little access to the world outside. And we were very suspicious of outsiders. But the world came to my door in these religious sessions organised by the VHP,' Dungar said. 'They told us they were going to change our lives. They said that if we ever got into trouble with the police, they would get us out. And they could, because there was always someone from the top level of the VHP who became a district-level neta, a politician.'

Before his association with the Sangh, if Dungar was ever in a fight with a Muslim, he was always at a disadvantage. Taking on one Muslim was like taking on a group. After he joined the VHP, the balance of power shifted. A fight erupted when people in Dungar's village saw a young Muslim auto-rickshaw driver do the unthinkable—have a Hindu girl sit beside him instead of in the passenger seat.

Later, the girl's brother confronted the driver. 'Why did you make her sit next to you?' he hollered.

The driver replied, 'Because there was no space at the back.'

The brother shot back, 'That's a lie. The passenger seat was empty.'

He beat up the driver. The stage was set for a Hindu–Muslim confrontation.

For the next four days, nothing happened. Then a group of Muslims from the driver's village got together and retaliated. They beat up four or five Hindu boys. Dungar talked about this at a VHP meeting he attended that evening, and things changed immediately. The Hindus regrouped, and Dungar saw for the very first time how the Muslims from the area were outnumbered.

From then on, the VHP put their weight behind Dungar, and he had to display his loyalty to the Sangh in return. The time it mattered most was during the Babri masjid campaign in Ayodhya. By this time, Dungar was in college. He had registered under the open-university scheme so he wouldn't have to attend classes. There was no question that he needed to work, but Dungar felt that if he also pushed himself to get a college degree, he would be permanently rid of the cycle of debt and penury that a dwindling crop and reduced land-holding imposed on him. But it was a punishing choice. To pay for college, he had to take on two, sometimes three jobs simultaneously.

For a few months, Dungar signed up to be a security guard. He had to report for work at 6 p.m. and stay up until 2 a.m. Often, he found himself being shaken out of a deep sleep by the thumping of his supervisor's bamboo stick. It was hard to keep his eyes open at night after the day job at a construction site. Dungar dropped the security job and invested his savings of Rs 27,800 in a corn-grinding machine. He set up a tiny shop in the village and pounded the village's supply of corn into cornflour for a fee. The irony of this wasn't lost on him. 'I was doing the same work as a completely uneducated person,' he pointed out.

It would all be worth it if the new enterprise could help him jump levels to a status and position where he would never have to do this kind of work again. The VHP and BJP would help with that, Dungar was certain. He went along with thousands of volunteers to attend a rally in Delhi. It was a big show of strength in the build-up to the Ayodhya campaign. However, on 6 December 1992, the day of reckoning, Dungar had college exams and was unable to go. But he could not afford to let the VHP down, so he sent a team of twenty-six volunteers instead. 'Down with the Muslims. Down with the mosque,' they chanted. Dungar tracked the events from his village as news trickled in through word of mouth and rumours.

Everyone heard of the successful mission. Of the thousands of Hindus who swarmed Ayodhya as if a giant beehive had been shaken out. Of the Hindu leaders in saffron clothes who climbed on top of the sixteenth-century minaret, urging the crowd to follow suit. And then, right in the middle of the Sangh Parivar's biggest powder-keg moment, Dungar was suddenly exposed to its cold, calculated inner workings. His team of twenty-six didn't make it to Ayodhya, or even the state of Uttar Pradesh. They were offloaded instead in a high-school building in an altogether different state—in the Ratlam district of Madhya Pradesh. Someone had apprehended trouble and diverted the volunteers. They were made to wait in an abandoned school for three days with no money or proper arrangements for food, and no word sent home to their worried families. They eventually made it back to Gujarat, tired and very angry.

Having sent them there, it was now Dungar's job to pacify them. He made note of the VHP's volte-face and put the information aside for the moment. This was not the time to dwell on the bits of the story that didn't add up. The group had raised his profile considerably. Everyone in his village and the adjoining villages knew who he was. And the success of the Babri mission ran through the village like a fever. It turned the political complexion of the entire district a very Hindu saffron. In the state election that followed the demolition in 1995, an overwhelming majority voted for the BJP.

In the midst of this successful transition to a better social status, there was one part of his past that Dungar could not successfully erase. He had to marry a girl chosen by his parents as soon as he finished class ten. She was from the village adjoining his. With so much pressure on him when he was not even eighteen, Dungar had to make sure that his carefully built alliances delivered what he needed them to: an opportunity to escape the cycle of debt, manual labour and living on the edge.

NINE

For Pranav, the year that the Babri masjid was demolished
was significant for a very different reason. It was the year
he saw his first cricket World Cup on TV. In his world, life
was mapped in cricket matches. Afternoons were measured
in the number of overs left in a game. There was no TV at
home, but there was one at the village council, or panchayat
ghar. In World Cup season, that was where life began and
ended. Even now, talking about it makes Pranav's eyes shine.
It was a historic edition for many reasons. For the first time
in twenty years, the embargo imposed on South Africa for its
apartheid regime was lifted. It was the first time that cricket
players wore coloured jerseys. And the cup was eventually
lifted for the first time by a country many in the expanding
Hindu right considered the Enemy. The Muslim-majority
state of Pakistan.

Since the Partition of 1947, Pakistan has always had a
larger-than-life presence in the minds of Indians. The big day
to watch out for was the India–Pakistan face-off in Sydney.
Watching cricket at the panchayat ghar was an all-male affair.
The large hall where the screening took place was little more
than a semi-open veranda. Its brick-tiled roof was propped
up on pillars and the rest was open to the elements. The sides
had been covered with thick cloth to prevent the bright sun
from streaming in and rendering the TV screen invisible. On

the day of the match, the hall was overflowing with people. Kids were not allowed, but that was perfectly alright. Pranav and his friends found a favourite peephole where the cloth cover was torn. Test cricket went on for five or six hours, and they didn't really want to be seated silently in the hall. Watching, or rather, listening from outside was much better. 'Oh there, it's a sixer, it's a six,' someone screamed. And they kept track while playing their own match right outside.

On this day, the anticipation and silence in the room was deafening. When India won, the hall erupted in loud, raucous conversation. This was the part Pranav liked most. 'When India won, there would be long discussions for a few hours after. If we lost, everyone just went home quietly.'

India won against Pakistan by a comfortable margin of forty-three runs, but the joy was short-lived. The team crashed out in the quarter-finals, losing to the West Indies. But this was the World Cup. Even with India no longer in the reckoning, it was important to keep score of the big wins and losses. Pakistan made it to the finals, and were scheduled to play against England.

On the day of the match, Pranav found to his surprise that most people in the village were on Pakistan's side. When Pakistan won the title and the team captain Imran Khan held up the shiny silver cup on TV, everyone around was celebrating.

He was confused. Weren't Pakistanis meant to be shunned, like most things Muslim? This seemed like surprisingly contrarian behaviour, so he asked an elder what the jubilation was about. 'Until the finals, no one in our village was supporting Pakistan,' Pranav said. 'Then, in the finals, they were the only Asian country left. Toh I heard people saying that we should support Pakistan. I said, kyun? Some

said because India isn't in the finals in any case, but at least
the cup should stay in Asia.' Momentarily then, enmities
could be put aside for the sake of cricket.

Later that year, there was Babri.

Even as a fourteen-year-old, Pranav sensed that something
big was about to happen. Every house got involved in the
campaign to build a Ram temple in place of the mosque. The
excitement was much greater than the World Cup. 'It wasn't
one day or one month,' Pranav explained. 'It was a four- or
five-month process.'

He saw it build up as each house donated a brick
to the building of the temple. The village elders chose a
representative to carry the bricks to Ayodhya. The man
chosen for the mission was a sixty-five-year-old who went
from 'nothing to a hero', Pranav recalled, a mocking smile
on his face. When the man in question was all set for his
journey, the village gathered around and gave him a few
extra bricks to put into his satchel in case the cartload they
had put together was waylaid. Everyone pooled in money
for his trip, and gave him a warm and auspicious send-off.

For some time, there was no news of the bricks or what
had happened to the man. Where was he? Pranav wanted
to know, but had to put a lid on his curiosity until the man
returned. Meanwhile, everyone had to make do with what
they saw on TV and in the papers. News came in that the
mosque had come down, and that there was violence in
many parts of the country, including Gujarat. The next day,
newspapers reported that 246 people had died in religious
clashes. Most were Muslims. Pranav's village had remained
untouched, and everyone was waiting eagerly for their
representative. He finally made it back, armed with a video
recording of the events. It was a propaganda tape that the

VHP had allowed him to borrow for a day, to screen in the village as a celebration of victory and also as evidence of his visit.

The screening turned into quite an event. It was organised in the home of the local cable TV operator. 'People said the screening should be held in the cable guy's house so that it would be limited to a select group of people. If the whole village gathered around, then the police would get to know. And there could be trouble,' Pranav said. The undercover nature of the event put him in a privileged position because his house was close to the cable TV operator's. The screening was only for adults, but Pranav and his friends found a way to get in. 'We went and sat in the guy's house much in advance. Slowly people started to trickle in for the screening. There were forty or fifty people.'

The screening turned out to be anticlimactic. There were reams and reams of footage of boring speeches by leaders Pranav didn't know or care about. He was looking for one thing only. A picture of the sixty-five-year-old representative from his village. Where was he in these endless shaky shots? Precisely nowhere. In the melee of thousands, there wasn't even one microscopic millionth of a second of screen time with him in it. 'It was not very exciting. But then we said, chalo, at least we got to see what was going on, what had happened,' Pranav recalled.

Meanwhile, in the real world, there were bigger issues for him to contend with. Having struck out against his father in his determination to study the arts, there was no one to turn to for advice on what to do next or where and how.

The first tentative step Pranav took was to become an English teacher. His English was better than that of most others in the village, so he enlisted for a bachelor's degree by correspondence, and gave English language and grammar lessons in the evening to earn some money. After the upheaval he had caused with his defiance, there was relative calm at home. Two more or less uneventful years went by. Then a friend advised Pranav to take a leap of faith and consider enrolling in a more prestigious college far from home, in a big city.

There was the obvious lure of independence and better prospects at work. And crucially, a chance to see what he was really made of, shorn of the protective umbrella of his parents and the closed circle they occupied in the village. Pranav decided to visit the college and then make up his mind.

The campus was a mini-universe in its own right, spread out and diverse, with people from all over the state and quite a few from other parts of the country. And the city was teeming with independent hostels and student canteens. There were large and little dhabas, chai shops, sandwich shops and dosa joints, with bikes parked carelessly in front, blocking the entrance. Young men with defiantly held cigarettes chatted with women wearing jeans as emancipation. Their eagerness rose above the constant hum of city traffic. Pranav was instantly hooked. Away from home and his father, working his way into a new city life. This was where he wanted to be.

TEN

Suresh was working his way into the life of a young Muslim girl who had just moved with her family to Naroda Patiya. Fourteen-year-old Farzana was entirely unaware of his publicly proclaimed resolve to marry a Muslim as revenge. Everyone in the area had their eye on her. Her wilful, kohl-lined eyes looked directly at whomever they pleased, defying all the usual codes prescribed for women—that they must lower their gaze, be deferential. Her pretty pout underlined a lurking free spirit that was beginning to drive the men in the twin neighbourhoods of Chharanagar and Naroda Patiya crazy. Farzana was followed wherever she went. It made the prospect of luring her into his trap even more exciting for Suresh. She was highly coveted.

He first laid eyes on Farzana while working himself into a sweat with a punishing number of push-ups. Farzana and her sister walked past him in the direction of a wedding party that was packing up for the night. Even in the dark, Farzana's eyes shone. It was 10.30 p.m., and Suresh decided to follow them. The two sisters picked up the scent of someone on their trail, and ran back home as fast as they could. It was scary because they were in unfamiliar territory, having moved to Naroda Patiya only recently. The move had followed a deeply unsettling phase of being out on the street and destitute, the result of a family dispute. Farzana, her sisters and mother had spent the last year and a half shunting between relatives and acquaintances, and even had a brief stint living in a graveyard, after the grandmother—their father's mother—kicked them out of their home. The father had ditched his family to stay on with the grandmother. Living on the street with no patriarch to protect them made the girls especially vulnerable. Farzana was always looking over her shoulder. Now, she ran straight to her sister's husband, out of breath as she said between gasps, 'We're being followed.'

To her utter amazement, the man following them turned up at their doorstep, now dressed in a formal shirt, and greeted her brother-in-law. Her brother-in-law, who seemed to know and trust Suresh, asked, 'These two have been followed by two men, have you any idea who it could be?' Suresh pretended to look nonplussed, and said he had absolutely no idea. He had noted that this was where the girl lived. From that day on, he stalked Farzana regularly. He was there when she went to the grocer's shop to buy grain, or to the goat-herder for milk. And most often, when she headed to the common well or handpump to fill water. There was no water supply in the homes in Naroda Patiya, so everyone queued up to fill their buckets in the morning and evening. It was the one spot where Farzana felt most vulnerable, since it was essential to be there at the same time of day, every day. That meant encountering the persistent, lascivious gaze of many men who seized the opportunity to make a pass at her and get in her way. Suresh took it upon himself to be her protector. It allowed him to display his might to potential competitors and impress her at the same time. After nearly two years of living on the streets and being surrounded by men who tried to grab her, a gym-going, chest-thumping protector was a huge relief. 'If anyone troubles you, just let me know. I'm usually at my friend's place right across the road,' Suresh said reassuringly.

Over the next few months, they started to see a lot of each other. Suresh was muscular and charming. He had a penetrating gaze that could be menacing at one moment and desperately seeking love the next. Suresh made sure Farzana saw this side of him. He even called her over to his house to make rotis for his diabetic mother. An affinity developed between the two women. One afternoon, Farzana had gone over to Suresh's and his mother wasn't home. She was wearing a smart salwar kameez, the colour of chikoo fruit. Suresh sat down next to her and held her hand. Before she could pull away, he held her other hand, leaned over and kissed her. Suddenly, the world around her melted away, and there were only the two of them. 'I felt in that one moment that, come what may, I will be with this man forever,' she said.

Farzana was living in a movie. Specifically, in the movie *Qayamat Se Qayamat Tak* (From One Apocalypse to the Next). Suresh added to the filminess by declaring to Farzana, 'I love you. I love your eyes. They are just like Hema Malini's.' Was he merely acting according to plan, or was he also, despite himself and his cold resolve, falling in love? Either way, it was clear by now that Farzana had more or less made up her mind, even though she was aware of the violence within the man she was smitten by. She witnessed it first-hand while visiting her sister's house, where she saw Suresh pulverising a man next door. The man had apparently gone home drunk and beaten his wife. Suresh decided to act as a self-styled vigilante and teach him a lesson by beating him black-and-blue with a wooden baton. Years later, a man from the area who saw it all happen, looked back and remarked, 'Suresh occupied Farzana's world so completely that there was no room for any of us to warn her about what he was like.'

But her mother warned Farzana about getting involved with Suresh. 'When he can do this to the neighbour, what will prevent him from beating you up?' she said.

By then, it was already too late. 'He's just a little angry, that's all, Ammi,' Farzana said. 'He'll change, he'll soften over time.'

Perhaps this was what she had been telling herself since she fell in love with Suresh. But it was equally true that Farzana was no stranger to violence. The neighbourhood she had grown up in—Ram Rahim Ka Tekra in Jamalpur—was a lot like Chharanagar. It was an unkempt shanty subject to the whims of competing mafia groups that dealt in petty crime, drugs, liquor and real estate. After dark, young boys peddled hooch and older men bent over carrom boards and gambled. The odd expletive punctuated the evening air as fights broke out between couples over money, or even just the plain, unforgiving heat. Farzana's mother was often subject to the ugly temper and curse words of her father. The scale may have been different from what she saw in Chharanagar with Suresh, but for fourteen-year-old Farzana, violence wasn't a deal breaker.

What could have gotten in the way was another man, with whom her brother-in-law had arranged a match. The boy's parents liked Farzana. He came from a respectable family with prospects of a stable income. And she came from the Saiyyad clan, an aristocratic Muslim caste. It didn't matter that Farzana lived in a slum. And she was positively arresting to look at, so her parents reasoned that there would be no dearth of good suitors. The boy came to meet Farzana one evening and asked to take her out on his bike for a cold drink.

Her parents approved, and they went to a roadside dhaba and ordered Thums Up. As they sipped their tangy colas, the boy looked up at Farzana and confessed, 'I am in love with someone else.' She was aghast. It seemed extraordinary, in fact preposterous, from her point of view that he should say this; it was his family that had approached hers in the first place. She was perfectly aware of her looks and status. She came home and declared to her mother, 'Now I will not marry any Muslim man. That's that.' She decided soon after to marry Suresh.

Her parents wouldn't hear of it. Farzana's father had moved in with the rest of the family by this time, and he kept his daughter under house arrest when he found out about her relationship. But it was too late. Suresh had already become a constant. He cast such a dark shadow over the family that it made their landlord uncomfortable. The landlord asked them to leave. This was exactly what Suresh had planned. If he arranged for her family to be evicted from Naroda Patiya, they could be relocated to Chharanagar, where Farzana would always be within sight.

One afternoon, when she had gone to fill water from the common well, Suresh whisked Farzana away and took her to meet his uncle. The uncle took one look at her and remarked, 'But this is not the girl whose photo you showed me. That was someone else you wanted to marry, wasn't it?' Farzana froze with incomprehension. It turned out that Suresh had been two-timing Farzana with her own sister. He had intended to marry the sister, and had even shown her photograph to his chacha for approval. But the sister had turned Suresh down when he proposed to her. Farzana was only Plan-B.

Farzana ran home devastated, crying and then fighting

her tears to prevent her family from seeing the torment. She could not sleep. The following day, she sent word through a friend to Suresh, asking him to meet her at the local dairy. She had to find out what his true intent was. If she was to end her romance, she needed to confront him and then make up her mind. Farzana sneaked out of the house when her father was asleep on the charpai, telling her mother she was going to buy dahi. At the dairy, though, she was confronted not by her romantic hero but a menacing man with a knife. Suresh grabbed her by the scruff of her neck, held a knife at her throat and said, 'You come away with me right now and marry me, or I will plunge this into your stomach and then go after your family.'

Now that the elder sister had turned him down, Suresh needed Farzana to marry him to save face. He did not intend to leave her with any choice. Therefore, the knife. Meanwhile, word went out that her parents had found her missing from home and concluded that she must have run away with Suresh. They filed a case with the police, accusing him of kidnapping their daughter, who was seventeen and still a minor. Suresh was informed that the police was on the lookout for the couple. They had to run. He told Farzana that he had family in Rajasthan and that is where they would go. There was a distinct possibility that they would be able to get married there, since child marriages were common in the state. Suresh dragged Farzana with him to the bus station, and they made their way out of Gujarat.

Now Farzana was on a bus with a man who had wanted to marry her sister. She was estranged from her parents, and the movie-like romance she had conjured up was dashed to pieces. They arrived at Suresh's aunt's house in the district of Balotra. By now, the police was looking all over Chharanagar and Naroda Patiya for Suresh. At his aunt's house, Farzana had to remain undercover while Suresh skulked about town trying to organise a court wedding. A few weeks later, he informed Farzana that he had succeeded. The papers were made out. All she had to do was sign and change her name to a Hindu one that he had picked out for her—Seema. The full name she signed on to in the affidavit was Seema Suresh Jadeja. Wife of Suresh Jadeja. They headed back home to Chharanagar.

ELEVEN

Dungar, who was staying at the students' hostel at the time, went back home to get married. It was a thoroughly confusing time. Although he had carefully carved out a space for himself as an active member of the Sangh Parivar, the wedding was a rude reminder that he wasn't as emancipated as he had imagined. He was fifteen when his father decided it was time for him to do what everyone else in the village did at his age. What made following this time-honoured tradition so difficult was precisely that one thing—time. Once upon a polygamous time, his father could have seven wives, and that was not unusual. It was one way of acknowledging his attraction for all those women and accounting for it publicly. Adolescents were married young to check raging hormones, and to keep the inheritors and inheritance from being scattered.

By the middle of the 1990s, however, Dungar had adopted the Sangh Parivar's homogenised Hindu identity wholesale. He now believed that marriage was a status-defining marker. That it had to be arranged in such a way that a man married up to a superior social or financial status. It was required to be solemnised by brahmins chanting Sanskrit shlokas—and, in the modern context, the couple in question must both be adults.

Living away from home had helped him dodge marriage for a while, but he could not evade his family forever. 'I said

I didn't want to get married, but my uncle forced me to. My father's elder brother.' Dungar confessed, 'I was young and so scared of him. I felt completely trapped.' The ceremony was suitably aspirational and conducted by two brahmins called from the nearby town, as the village had none. Once it was done, Dungar found a way out of his predicament. He used his superior status as a man to ignore his wife completely. She stayed home with his parents while he moved back to the hostel to complete his higher secondary schooling.

'It made me sad, the whole marriage thing, and I didn't even live with her, with my wife,' he said. He barely acknowledged her even when she was pregnant and had their first child, then the second and third. He moved back home only two years later, when it was time to go to college. The only way forward that Dungar could see for himself was to push as hard as it was physically possible to do. Better finances would give him some power to talk back to his family, and disregard what he had been forced into. He enrolled in a bachelor's degree by correspondence. Alongside, he took on one, sometimes two jobs to pay for it and provide for his new expanded family. 'Those were very tough times,' Dungar said, looking thoughtful.

Then it started to get better. Dungar was learning to be a machinist along with everything else. And he had enrolled in a vocational course at the nearest ITI, Industrial Training Institute. One day, on his way to the institute, he ran into a man who helped him access a completely new universe of money and power.

The man was a local tribal affairs officer who lived in the adjoining town. He asked Dungar, 'What do you do?'

The reply was impressive. Dungar told the man, Rameshbhai,* his whole routine. 'I start out at 5.30 each morning, get on the bus to town for my ITI class and work as a turner-fitter, assembling industrial parts. Then I get home at 2 p.m. to spend the next few hours running the corn-grinding machine. I also take on construction jobs on contract from time to time.'

After listening to him, Rameshbhai said, 'Why don't I give you some work? Will you come see me in my office?'

Dungar wasn't sure what to expect. He had tried every possible avenue for upward mobility—from filling out forms to join the security forces to attempts at joining the police—and landed nowhere. He was weary.

'What work will it be?' he asked.

Rameshbhai assured him this was different. 'It will be work that uses up all these government schemes put out there for the benefit of tribals,' he said.

Now Dungar was interested. 'I turned up the very next day,' he said, looked pleased. 'He had all these forms to be filled out. Apparently tribals could get tubewells built for free, or bullock carts, engine oil, camels—there was all sorts of stuff on offer.'

It was funny how Dungar had been running from his tribal identity all this while only to run into someone who was telling him to hold on to it. And use it to extract every last drop in a world that had turned entirely transactional. He returned with five forms that he quickly got people in the village to fill up. The next time it was fifteen, then twenty forms. For every form filled out and every scheme availed of, Rameshbhai gave Dungar a cut. Money started to pour in. 'I was doing three things simultaneously,' Dungar said. 'I put other people on the job, of course, and I would supervise it all. I would get people to help distribute and fill out forms for all the welfare schemes, then I would do the turner-fitter job in the day and then grind corn in the evenings.'

Then, one day, Rameshbhai suggested to Dungar that he institutionalise his tribal welfare work. 'Why don't you set up a trust?' It sounded unreal. This was the opportunity Dungar had been waiting for his whole life. To make enough money that he would not need to stoop over the corn crop, sickle in hand, season after season. Or stand in front of his grinding machine drenched in corn-ash and sweat. This could be a permanent way out. He ran from one office to the next, bribing the correct officers everywhere into giving him his scheduled tribe certificate. In all these machinations, the Sangh Parivar's were the invisible hands that moved the bureaucratic machine and got the officers to sign on the dotted line.

Dungar set up the Vanvasi Kalyan Sangathan.* The Forest Dwellers' Association. In its creation, there was a strangely poetic irony. It wore an outer shell of being adivasi—set up for the welfare of tribals—whilst going against the essence of that term. The association's Ghar Chalo Abhiyan was an invitation to return to a universal Hindu fold, dressed in decorative tribal cover.

Putting some distance between him and the traditions that had forced him into an uncomfortable marriage was personally freeing for Dungar. There was also the dazzling promise of something more powerful than his immediate environment could provide. His friends in the village had also begun to feel the force. As for Dungar, he was already someone to reckon with. The VHP with its slap-on Hindu identity gave him power. It was also a powerful marketing machine.

As the head of the VHP for the entire block, Dungar's target was to sign on 10,000 new members. He signed on 12,000. 'I was the number one performer in the entire block. I was very proud of that,' Dungar said. At a meeting in Ahmedabad later that year, he was commended highly for his enthusiasm and efficiency. In return, he was tasked with signing on even more members and organising their indoctrination into the Sangh's more militant arm, the Bajrang Dal.

The ceremony had enough testosterone to charge the new recruits Dungar brought in. Everyone had to pay Rs 150, and in return they were each given a shiny silver-coloured trishul—a sharp trident—to wield. A priest was called in to recite shlokas in Sanskrit. And the group of 150 new recruits held up these tridents and took a pledge. The district head of the VHP led the way: 'I will protect all Hindus. I will protect the holy cow—our mother—and I will protect our mothers and sisters.' The last was understood by all to mean that women would be 'saved' from Muslim and Christian men.

The leader went on to make a speech. 'These trishuls, they are poison-tipped. When they pierce through flesh, poison enters the bloodstream and it makes the nerves swell up. If you drive this into the stomach of your enemy, it will rip their insides out.' He built up a fever pitch before driving home the main point. 'These trishuls are not to be used against Hindus. But when the time comes, you will need to attack Muslims.'

Dungar was excited. The crowd of people who had just taken oath were all under his command. 'We went around defending the faith against Muslims transporting cows for slaughter,' Dungar explained. 'We positioned ourselves along the main road and stopped trucks carrying cows. We would say—come on, get down from that truck now.' He added, 'I rescued about fifteen cows. It felt great. My chest swelled with pride.'

In the years leading up to 2002, Dungar deployed two or three men on the thoroughfare whose job it was to defend the faith against potential cow-slayers. This was a lookout team baying for Muslim blood, and eager to pounce.

TWELVE

In Chharanagar, the police apprehended Suresh for the kidnapping of Farzana—a minor and now his wife. It was the middle of 1996. After three months on the run in Rajasthan, Suresh felt he was equipped to deal with the police, armed as he was with marriage papers stamped by a local court. He brought Farzana back home. They had had been a long and exhausting day, and were fast asleep when there was a sharp rap on the door. It was 2 a.m. when Farzana woke up with a start. She opened the door to find herself face to face with the police. The men had come for Suresh, but when they didn't see him, they grabbed her hand, knowing that it would definitely bring him to the door. Farzana screamed and he rushed out, still half asleep and livid to see strange men in his home. The police had arrived in plainclothes. Suresh gave them no time to explain who they were. He assumed they were a local gang and beat them up. It was only when they hit back that Suresh discovered he had messed with the wrong people. They thrashed him relentlessly, breaking the bones in his arm and then locking him up for a few days.

Despite the unpromising start, once Suresh was back home, he seemed devoted to his wife. Farzana was beginning to think she hadn't made a bad choice of husband after all. Her in-laws treated her like she was their own daughter. Since she was just fifteen years old, Suresh's mother would sit her down and comb her long black hair into two plaits like she would have done for a schoolgirl. The parents made it their business to teach her Bhantu—the language the Chharas spoke—bit by bit. 'They compensated so well for the fact that I had cut myself off from my family,' she recalled. It didn't last.

'Here's that son of mine who went and married a Qajji,' she heard Suresh's father say, completely drunk. 'What will the neighbours say? How will I get my other two sons married?'

Farzana bristled with anger as she shot back, 'Your son brought me here, I didn't come of my own accord.' She went across to Suresh's chachi Radhaben and asked for support.

Radhaben was fond of Farzana, so she stepped in and told the parents, 'Now that your son has brought home a Muslim, you've got to keep her, na!'

But Suresh did not stand up for Farzana. On the contrary, he was incensed that she had decided to talk back to his father. 'You don't open your mouth, you hear me?' he hollered at her. A few days later, the message would be hammered home with an iron fist. Suresh came home drunk. When he sat down to a late dinner, he found that the food had too much salt. 'I had never set foot in a kitchen before I was married. So I wasn't particularly good at cooking,' Farzana recalled. Suresh flung the plate away, then dragged Farzana by her hair out of the house to the backstreet, in full view of the window to her mother's room, which overlooked that street. He beat her repeatedly and mercilessly. Then the anger vanished just as quickly as it had appeared, and was followed by an equal dose of remorse. Suresh fell at Farzana's mother's feet, sobbing. 'Please forgive me, Ammi, this will never happen again,' he pleaded.

What made Farzana's predicament confusing were the

days when Suresh's other side was on display. Then he said,
'When you are out of sight for even a minute, I go nuts. I
love you very much.' He took her to the movies. 'He also only
wore what I picked out for him. All his clothes were what I
chose,' Farzana said of those times. They went to a fair where
they had identical tattoos made on their wrists. One was of
the Khodiyar Mata, the mother goddess that many Chharas
were devotees of. It was a big green tattoo of the goddess
riding on a crocodile. Another was of their initials—S and
S for Suresh and Seema, her married name, and also S and
F for Suresh and Farzana. Their names locked together in
permanence and encased in an arrow-pierced heart.

However twisted Suresh's love seemed, Farzana was
certain it was love, because it was accompanied by another
telltale ingredient, jealousy. He could not stand to have
Farzana praised by another. A stray comment from a
neighbour, 'I love your wife's clothes,' was enough to set him
off. 'Do you dress for me or for everyone on the street?' he
would say, grabbing Farzana's clothes, ripping them off her
and cutting them to pieces.

Fear and jealousy were both bottomless pits. One night,
not too long after their marriage, he reached home late and
knocked on the door several times. It took a while for Farzana
to open it, by which time Suresh was certain his worst fears
had come true. 'Who were you fucking that it took you
so long to come to the door?' he thundered. Nothing
Farzana said could stop the tirade. 'I was fast asleep, so I
didn't hear ...' Before she could finish, he had grabbed her
by the hair, pulled her to the backstreet once again, under the
window of her mother's house. He beat her repeatedly with
a lathi. Suresh did not stop until his mother and younger
brother intervened, and physically held him back.

Farzana's mother took her aside. 'Look, what's happened has happened,' she said, trying desperately to reason with her. 'People in Jamalpur don't know about this elopement of yours. We can all go back there and forget you ever married him.' Before Farzana had time to think over what her mother had suggested, Suresh was at the door, remorseful again and begging both Farzana and her mother to forgive him. But his pleas were overturned almost immediately by the arrival of his mother on the scene. She jumped to Suresh's defence, insulting Farzana even as her son was bent over in apology. 'These Muslim women are paid for. They make money from sleeping around, they can never stick to one man,' she hissed. It turned into an ugly battle between the two mothers-in-law. But in the end, Farzana had made up her mind. Her spirit was broken and she had concluded that it was her fate to live with this man, no matter how terrible the odds. They had consummated the marriage, and that, as far as she was concerned, was the end of the road for her. There would be no question of finding another man. She told her mother, Khatoonbibi, to stop defending her. She didn't want her mother to be humiliated by Suresh's family anymore. 'I will stay right here,' she said to her mother. 'This is my fate.'

It was too much for Khatoonbibi to take. If her daughter had made up her mind to stay, then she and the rest of the family would have to leave Chharanagar. That would be easier than watching her daughter suffer every day. Khatoonbibi made up with her mother-in-law by telling her that Farzana's plight was the result of their banishment. It could happen to the other sisters too if they didn't move back. So they did. The family returned to Jamalpur and agreed that, from then on, there would be no further communication with Farzana or Suresh. Their girl had chosen that hell and she would have to burn in its purgatory fire alone.

In her isolation, Farzana had no choice but to focus on her adoptive family—Suresh's parents, his chacha–chachi and other relatives in Chharanagar. What she began to realise, although it was no consolation, was that Suresh's violence was not directed exclusively at her. Its volcanic molten mass was hurled in all directions and at everyone he interacted with, including his parents. It plugged into a lifetime of humiliation Suresh relived each time he was publicly ridiculed by his father. The line he used on Farzana so often— 'Who have you been fucking'—echoed what Suresh's father said to his mother. 'I don't know who that woman fucked to produce a son like this. He's not mine.' The father's words had framed the life of not just one but two of the children. It also became the dominant narrative for Suresh's younger brother Vinoo, formally known as Vinod. Farzana saw that when Vinoo was drunk and fighting with his wife, he recycled the same accusation. 'You were sleeping with someone else ... this baby isn't mine.' Vinoo's wife eventually left him.

Would Suresh have treated Farzana differently if she wasn't Muslim? Would it have helped if she hadn't been so beautiful? There were no answers. It did not help at all that she had begun to be turned off by Suresh. As much as she shunned him sexually, he wanted her even more. Farzana submitted but at the same time held her own, taking no pleasure in it at all. 'I would turn my face away when he came on to me,' she explained. In response he would say, 'You just lie there like a corpse.' He would come away feeling even more bruised and suspicious of his wife. She must love another, he was convinced.

By the time she was seventeen and Suresh about thirty, they were expecting their first child. Farzana, still a child herself, was in a fair bit of pain. Her body had not filled out enough to accommodate a new being. The doctor suggested she abort the baby. But Suresh wouldn't hear of it. His mother patted Farzana on the head, and said to her gently, 'Don't worry. It will all be okay.'

Of course, it wasn't okay. Suresh made sure of that. He turned to Farzana one day and declared, 'You had better not be having a girl. If you do, I will kill both you and the baby. Is that clear?' As if a threat could will the genetics of the child. Farzana was paralysed with fear as Suresh's aunt took her to the hospital when she was due. When the baby was delivered, the nurse informed her that it was a girl. The colour drained from Farzana's face.

Suresh's chachi asked at once, 'What's the matter? Why are you shaking like this?'

Farzana told her about Suresh's threat.

'What rubbish,' the older woman said confidently. 'Do you think he will have the gumption to raise a finger at you or the baby? I am taking you home right now to my house.'

Farzana had no choice. There was no communication with her parents. She had nowhere else to go.

It turned out the aunt was right. For the first few days, Suresh sat beside his wife and child with a sullen face, refusing to look at them, but causing them no harm. On the sixth day, a puja was performed for the well-being of the child. Suresh held his daughter for the first time. It triggered something massive in him. 'I have had an aversion to girls ever since my sister let me down by running away with a Muslim man,' he said to Farzana in what seemed to her to be part confession, part admonition. At least it was communication. Words instead of violence. Maybe the baby had played her part. Suresh narrated the story of how he had married Farzana as an act of revenge, and told her that was why he didn't want to look at the face of their baby girl. When he finished speaking, he held her and suddenly, he was a father in love with his daughter. He named her Richie after his hero, refashioning the name of his West Indian cricketing god so Vivian Richards would pass his magic on. 'Richieeeeeeeee,' Suresh lisped. 'Richchuuuuuuu.'

He spent as much time with his daughter as possible. 'I will not let even the shadow of anything dark come near her,' he said to Farzana. 'She is my pet, my doll.' Suresh would take Richie with him to the Khodiyar Mata temple on the main road of Chharanagar on Sundays. And to the tiny photo studio around the corner to have her pictures taken.

Two years later, Farzana was pregnant again and Suresh's threat was renewed. 'This time it had better be a boy, or don't bother coming back.'

When the baby was born, a petrified Farzana looked up at the doctor and asked, 'What have I had doctor, a girl or a boy?'

The doctor replied, 'What did you want?'

Farzana looked wearily at him and said, 'A boy, or my husband will throw me out.'

The doctor informed her that it was indeed a boy.

Suresh burst into the hospital, ecstatic. He distributed pedas, the smell of sweet milk and cardamom spreading across the hospital ward as everyone ate one. And then he turned to Farzana and said, 'If it had been a girl, I would have given you some money and sent you away from here.'

They went home. Suresh, predictably, named the boy Vivian.* The boy fixation now dealt with, Farzana saw how Suresh's heart actually lay with his daughter. 'He went to the Baroda sub-jail on charges of thieving soon after Vivian was born, so he didn't get a chance to form a bond with him,' she clarified. Over time it became even more obvious that his daughter was the clear favourite. His wife was the favourite whipping boy.

The next major episode of violence erupted right after their son was born. Suresh had his breakfast and left the house for his usual round of thieving. When he got back, he discovered that his mother had also gone out to do her bit of robbery. That was the pretext for his explosion. 'How did you allow my mother out of the house?' he screamed at Farzana. Suresh's parents were professional thieves, but by the end of the 1990s, his mother had become diabetic and had been falling ill regularly. 'It's because you didn't go with her that she went out alone.' He pushed Farzana out into the street while she was holding their infant in her arms. Farzana's protestations, 'What could I have possibly said to stop your ammi?' fell on deaf ears. She took Vivian with her to the neighbour's house for the night.

'How could you turn her out in this state?' Suresh's chachi admonished him. 'What if she had died?'

Suresh replied, 'Well, if she were gone I wouldn't feel the loss at all.'

That was the night when the love Farzana had for Suresh slowly began to die.

THIRTEEN

Pranav was living a happy, free student life away from the disapproving gaze of his father. In college, unlike at home, he was liked for his confidence and rebelliousness. It took a massive earthquake in the year 2001 to shake him out of that bubble.

Gujarat was hit by an earthquake measuring 7.7 on the Richter scale. It was 8.46 a.m. precisely, and children in schools across the district of Kutch, the epicentre, were hoisting the national flag and singing the anthem to celebrate Republic Day. Many fell off the school building to their death. The devastation was enormous. Over 14,000 people died, and as many as 178 villages were flattened. Mountains of rubble formed a gnarled skyline, with people buried under. Some were half buried and shrieking for help. Pranav had just finished his bachelor of arts degree, and begun a master's in social science when the state appealed to his college, among many others, for help. Volunteers were needed to manage relief material, count the cost and generally reduce the stratospheric levels of stress. Kutch was a seven-hour bus ride away, but it offered the possibility of being able to do something immediately useful plus openings to a possible career in management or development. Pranav decided to sign up along with a few classmates. Three months of volunteer work in Kutch taught him what four years at university could not.

College had established Pranav as a clear leader. He was the guy people in class went to when the rule book needed some bending—in matters academic and thoroughly unacademic, like falling in love. One of the boys in Pranav's gang was drawn to a girl from the city. But there was a problem. City girls were meant to go out with local boys, and not dubious outsiders living in hostels. The city boys formed a formidable gang of fifty, and were proprietorial about the women in their sphere of influence, just like boys in feudal settings most anywhere in the country. It came down to a show of strength. Pranav's gang of six versus the local power group of fifty. There was a nervous recoil amongst his gangmates the day before as they wondered whether they shouldn't just back off. But Pranav declared coolly, 'Let them come for us, we'll deal with them.' He turned up with his friends the next evening in the local market. As the gang of fifty drew closer, Pranav approached them and said, 'Do what you want. We'll strike back.' Those words set something loose in the air. The locals backed off. They realised the group could hold its own.

Pranav's gang also realised just how much they depended on him. Most evenings, his room was the default adda, the place where the gang converged for food and drink. They were even caught with alcohol by the rector but wormed their way out of it with some dexterous handling of the police that came so naturally to Pranav. His classmates were amazed at how he consistently topped the class despite wandering aimlessly about town with them all year round. They did not see how deftly he could hide what was important to him.

When it came to volunteering in Kutch, it was this ability to get around the system, and also to organise and collate information, that came handy. Since everything had collapsed, from food supplies to water, electricity, drainage and housing, every bit of work made a big difference. 'It was an adventure for any college-going student,' Pranav said. 'We got a month off from college to volunteer there.' He was in a group that was in charge of distributing the relief packets that came in by the millions from various parts of the country to the collector's office. They had to be sampled, sorted, labelled and dispatched.

'It was very hard work,' Pranav said. 'We were told that we had to finish surveying the material in that particular zone in three days flat. It was at the border of Rapar in Kutch—six or seven villages that were far in the interior. We were at it continuously. When it got dark, we'd just fall asleep wherever we happened to be, alongside the people displaced from their villages. In the fields. There was of course no place to bathe or wash,' he remembered. 'We'd get back to our campus, rest for a day or two, have a bath and then feed all the information into our computer. It was fun.'

Kutch was also crawling with international aid workers—from the Red Cross and Oxfam to Christian, Jewish and Islamic aid organisations—and also media teams from all over the world. It gave Pranav an insight into the cruel and harsh world of aid that unfolded in the middle of the disaster. He saw that the speed at which a particular set of people got assistance depended on the access they had to power, and therefore to resources. The invisible matrix of caste and class that had held him up had suddenly become visible. There was no escaping those stark differences in the middle of this calamity. The exposure whetted Pranav's appetite. He had to see more, know more. When he saw that a senior from his MA class had found a job with an NGO in Kutch, Pranav told her determinedly, 'Keep space for me, please. I want to return in the summer break for a longer stint as a volunteer.' And he did.

He spent the next few months in some of the worst-affected blocks of Kutch—Samakhya, Bachau and Rapar. Ghost towns with monstrous grey piles of concrete. Amid the debris and decay, there was one observation Pranav made that stayed with him—the hyper-efficiency of a large army of volunteers from the RSS. The intellectual core of the Sangh Parivar. By their own admission, they were the largest volunteer group on the ground in Kutch, with an army of 25,000 people. No other group had numbers to match, or an internal dynamic that was so well synchronised. While big international NGOs were struggling to send food packets and water tanks and medicines to people, only the RSS was equipped to pick up dead bodies. They had learned lessons from another earthquake that had struck Latur in Maharashtra eight years earlier. They remembered the despair on the faces of so many as bodies decayed, compounding the loss and bereavement of those who lived. This time, whilst other aid agencies were focused primarily on rescue and rehabilitation, it was the RSS that was providing crucial psychological relief to people by holding a mass yagna ceremony on the thirteenth day of the quake, to lay to rest the souls of the dead.

'When the bodies were to be removed and cremated, there was no one else around except the RSS,' Pranav recalled. 'There was them, and then there were volunteers like me. So, when they said—come on, let's pull this body out, what should I have done? Should I have refused?' Pranav asked.

His short stint volunteering with the RSS made an impression on him at a crucial time. It was the year before 2002. So it was bound to be a reference point when the Sangh called upon Hindus to avenge the death of those who had been killed on the train.

THE TWENTY-EIGHTH AGAIN

FOURTEEN

28 February 2002 was a crucible. Everything and everyone was sucked into it, and after a molten breakdown, came out transformed. The idea that India should be recast from its secular mould into a Hindu nation was in the air for some time. But had it not been for the happenstance of the train-burning the day before and the madness after, the Hindu right would not have been able to marshal it to reshape the political landscape with the decisiveness that it did.

There was a way in which Pranav, Dungar and Suresh were wired by 2002 that perhaps made them more receptive than some to the tidal wave of hate that was unleashed. But it wasn't inevitable. What would have happened if, on the morning of the twenty-eighth, Suresh's brother had not been hit on the head with a soda bottle from the other side of the road? What if the Muslim man in Dungar's village had not fired empty bullets in the air, provoking his village into action? What if Pranav had decided not to watch vicariously as his mates looted the local Bata shop? On any day but 28 February, each of these instances may have amounted to sporadic, individual acts of violence. But on this day, Suresh's acts of killing Abdul Majid's family and Kauser Bano was a group act. Dungar's burning of the homes of Muslims was performed as a community rite. Pranav's bike rides were part of public voyeurism. More than fifteen districts of Gujarat worked as if they were one body mass. One fever. One ball of hate. It moved Hindu majoritarianism from an idea hovering on the political fringe to the centre stage.

Suresh's violence became emblematic of the most horrifying part of this political transformation. It forced everyone to confront the truth staring them in the face. Unless some people acted out in an extreme form, there no way to drive a sense of permanent fear into the minds of Muslims. For there to be fear, and for that fear to work as political currency, Suresh's uncontainable anger was necessary.

If that was all there was to be said about the essential nature of hate, it would be a tame story indeed. It would also be only Suresh's story. But the hate that 28 February announced contained many shades. What shade was Pranav, for instance, who was caught up in the tide of 2002 without purposefully hating at all? To look at his story is to see the many subconscious levels at which hate operates. How it finds a corner in the collective psyche of a people in such quiet ways that it seems like there is no story at all.

There is another crucial component of this anatomy that is, perhaps, the easiest to miss. Its ever-changing nature. That it was possible to be like Dungar, who had no firm opinion on Hindus and Muslims, or Hindus versus Muslims. Someone who used hate to propel his own meteoric rise without even knowing what it really was. Or what to do with it next. The phenomenon of hate is one that the Sangh Parivar would like to paint as fixed, because that is the only way for their politics to grow. But on closer inspection, we find that the minute we think we have nailed it, the anatomy changes on us.

This is the part of the story that, in most retellings of acts of violence, lies buried in the rubble along with the dead. There is an unconscious assumption that, once an act of mass violence takes place, the changes it effects are permanent. But that would be to undermine history, time and the nature of forging. For every new piece of metal, once laid out to cool and dry, starts to acquire a new life, new hues, new patinas, heat, dust, dirt and rust. And so it was with each of our protagonists over the fifteen years that followed.

AFTER

FIFTEEN

It was telling how a few hours of voyeurism would rob Pranav of his identity, his sense of self and all the small securities he had built his life around. Of being someone, belonging somewhere. It was a slow, significant unravelling.

In a few weeks, the anger sweeping across Gujarat died down. After initially looking the other way, the state finally stepped in to quell the violence, even as condemnation mounted from every side. Journalists and civil rights groups from New Delhi to New York accused the government of Gujarat of standing by with its eyes wide shut. They said that so many people across the state would not have been out on the streets unless they knew—as Pranav and his friends did—that the police would not touch them. So the state government finally did send the police and army in, and the mobs were forced to disband. Normal life of some sort could resume.

In college, Pranav's academic term was coming to an end, and it was time to submit a thesis to conclude his master's programme. While many of his classmates were scrambling for research subjects, Pranav had his ready three months ahead. He had not needed to think about it. The rubble from the earthquake and tents that stretched out like black bats had left an indelible imprint on his mind. The chaos and reordering of lives practically wrote themselves into his thesis. With classes over now, it was the deadest, dullest time of year. The university was deserted, the bike stands empty, the heat ever present and pointless like the day.

The monotony was broken briefly when friends asked Pranav for help. One friend in particular—Tanveer*—was struggling. He was Muslim and, with the atmosphere of fear still hanging thickly in the air, could not get out of his house. 'There was no way he could come to the campus and finish his thesis. His parents had told him they would rather he drop a year than risk his safety. He managed to get the message across to us, to the gang, that he needed help. He asked if we could pitch in and submit his thesis somehow,' Pranav said. A half-done version was lying with the local computer shop in the market close to college. No one had individual computers at the time. The entire MA class would converge on this shop and type out their hand-written thesis, or have it typed, printed and spiral-bound. 'We went to the shop and asked the owner to please allow us access to Tanveer's folder. We pored over the statistics and tables that were incomplete and submitted his thesis,' Pranav said.

It was time to look for a job. The campus had opened up to companies and NGOs for placements, but Pranav had no idea what he wanted to do. All he was certain of was that he did not want to be a cog in the wheel. 'I told my friends that I don't want a job. Jobs are for idiots. Why should I be anybody's slave?' Unfortunately, his summary dismissal of the plebeian pursuit of jobs wasn't known to a senior from college, who recommended him to her boss. In the evening, the phone rang in Pranav's dormitory, and the message was passed on that he had been shortlisted for an interview with a company the next day. 'I was confident that if I went, I would be selected,' he said, grinning. 'So I didn't go.' Such was Pranav's determination to stay out of the rat-race that he even turned down an offer set up by his teacher, who had scheduled an interview with a top corporate firm for the job of HR manager.

Now there was only one place to go—home. Pranav's parents were happy to see him. He had been living away for five years by this time. They said he should not feel like he had to hurry up and find a job. He could stay in the village and take his time. But in a few months, he was restless again. Having asserted his independence, it was hard to be back under the protective shadow of his father. Luckily, this didn't last very long. Pranav got a call from his friend Tanveer with a curious request. He needed help again. This time with the writing of a proposal for a project with an NGO. There was a catch. His project would only be considered if he formed a team of two—him plus one. And the team had to be a religiously syncretic one. Since he was Muslim, he needed to sign on a partner who was Hindu.

The relationship between Hindus and Muslims in the months after the violence of 2002 was so strained that stringing them together was like connecting two ends of a raw wire. Guaranteed to blow up the fuse box. That is why the NGO was trying an experiment to defuse the tension. Only those who successfully teamed up could get a foot in the door. Tanveer had no idea that Pranav had just been on the other side of the mob when he called him. The only thing he was focused on was making a water-tight proposal that the NGO would not be able to turn down. Since Pranav was a far better writer and, more importantly, had declared the need to do something of his own, Tanveer thought this would be just the thing for him.

'Yaar, please, help me write this proposal. If it gets

passed, we will be spearheading a very large project. You and I together,' Tanveer said. Pranav sat up at 'spearheading a project'. He said, 'We were told that if we came up with a workable plan, it would be turned into a full-fledged programme which we would be in charge of.' His eyes shone brighter, eyebrows arched in excitement as he went over that moment. But he had needed to know more. What kind of project was this? Tanveer explained. It was about resettling and rehabilitating Muslims displaced by the recent violence. Assessing the damage done, then repairing their homes.

Was fate playing some sort of trick on him? Throwing him the temptation of independence with the impossible challenge of working amongst the very people he had been brought up to despise? Pranav tried not to think about that. He assumed that the relief and rehabilitation work would be a lot like what he had done in Kutch. That it would be a large maze of chaos he could put his mind to. It would be fun.

There was one concern, though. He didn't trust Tanveer. Pranav had already bailed him out of many situations, including a sticky love affair with a Hindu girl. What would come of following him into a job? Tanveer had anticipated this, and had his answer ready: 'It won't be just me, you know. The company is recruiting lots of young people and asking them to form teams and pitch proposals.' Put like that, it sounded interesting, at least worth exploring. Pranav had just one more question. Where would the project be based? Tanveer said it would be in and around their university area. That sealed it. It was a semi-independent project, work he was familiar with and, best of all, in the place he had spent the last five years of his life. It would be like an extended college life, but with some money thrown in. What could be better? He agreed to do it, and went along with Tanveer to visit a few affected villages so he could write the proposal.

On the very first visit, Pranav realised that this was a very different kind of job from the one he had done during the earthquake. 'Our initial task was to survey the damage. And I discovered that there were so many villages where things were so bad that it was impossible to even enter. Like, in one village, eighty people had been killed. And in another, I had to go in alone,' Pranav said. 'It wasn't safe for Tanveer to come along. That's when I realised that this was not at all like your typical natural disaster type of situation, where people's houses are damaged and you repair them, and then things go back to normal. This wasn't like that.'

Pranav saw up close the single-mindedness with which the mob had acted in the village where eighty people were killed. They had led a group of Muslims to a three-storey house, assuring them that it was a safe place. Once the Muslim families had taken refuge there, the mob set the house on fire. Pranav returned from the visit with a head full of questions. 'I was asking myself, what next? And I got no answers. It didn't make sense. I mean, it's not like the entire Muslim population could be sent to Pakistan, right? So if they were out there living in camps and could not return home, then what would happen? And that question just led me to more questions. Would this lead to another cycle of violence? What if there was a counter attack, then this will never end. If we want this cycle to stop, we have to do something about it. But what?'

Pranav was also convulsed with fear. 'I was scared of the fact that I was a Hindu working for the rehabilitation of Muslims. If people around me figured this out, they would curse me no end,' he said. 'Obviously my friends were bound to find out. That scared me quite a bit. A lot of friends who did find out were asking me why I was working for Muslims, for those miya-log, when I could get any job I wanted.'

Pranav told himself that he could manage the difficult conversations with his friends. But there was an even bigger fear looming—that of dealing with the Sangh. 'At another level, I was thinking it would be equally bad if word got around to organisations like the VHP,' Pranav explained. 'So many people had rallied around their cause and loudly supported them. If they heard that I was working for the other side, I would be finished.'

There were days when Pranav found he was alone and alienated in his new work space. Tanveer and I went in a group of four or five, and we obviously went into Muslim neighbourhoods that were damaged by the violence. Suddenly, I would find I was standing alone, and a group of people would take Tanveer aside and talk to him.'

It was an impossible situation to be in. But the more he looked around, the more Pranav wanted to know. He went with Tanveer to a large relief camp. There were people everywhere, destitute, injured and bewildered: 25,000 of them. As far as the eye could see. 'I said to Tanveer—baap re! So many people, where did so many come from? This is a very scary and serious situation.' Tanveer replied that it was. And that there were entire villages with nobody left. Everyone had emptied out into camps.

There were already a number of NGOs distributing food, water and medical aid. Pranav and Tanveer's job was to help those who wanted to return home and get back on their feet. For now, they were living on food handouts. Women had made makeshift bathing spaces with pieces of cloth. Some were delivering babies there. Others had to go through their menstrual period with little or no access to water. From the stream of new and disturbing images he was exposed to, there was one in particular that Pranav found more difficult to process. The sight of a man crying—he was sobbing hysterically in full public view. 'I had never seen a man cry before,' Pranav said, not making eye contact. 'I thought women are meant to cry ... there's nothing out of the ordinary with that. But if a man was crying like this, something must be wrong somewhere with what these people had been put through.'

He tried to push that scene to the farthest corner of his mind and focus on the task at hand. Surveying villages. They made a list of 200 families across ten villages that wanted to return home. Until new homes could be built for them, the bosses told Pranav and Tanveer to prepare thirty-day survival kits. Rice, dal, kerosene, cooking oil, potatoes, red chilli powder, turmeric, salt and matchsticks. The everyday tasks were all-consuming, and left little time to think about the big picture. But there was no getting away from it—the contradiction between the horrors he saw and what he had grown up with. 'I had started to think that whatever had happened was very wrong. And that while it was all unfolding in February 2002, I had no idea. We were all just enjoying ourselves,' Pranav remarked.

Even if he wanted to look away, the NGO he worked for made sure that he could not. They held a workshop on the violence for all the new recruits, providing some perspective on where it came from. A slightly stout middle-aged man with an animated face addressed the group of twenty: eight Hindus, an equal number of Muslims and four Christians. He turned to his audience and asked, 'When you hear the word "Muslim", what comes to your mind first? Write this down on the card placed in front of you, without thinking, in the next thirty seconds.' Everyone bent down and scribbled their answers on the cards and handed them over to their mentor.

Pranav had written 'topiwalas—people with skullcaps' on his card. It was similar to the words the other Hindus in the room had put down: violent, bearded. The speaker went on to read out the list of words that the Muslims in the room had used to describe themselves. It was a study in contrasts. 'Pious, peace-loving' were some of their words.

The speaker turned to the class and asked them to think: how could both lists be true? 'I am not telling you what to believe,' he said. 'I want each of you to look at the word-lists and do some research. Look for evidence to support what you've written.'

He gave them an example. 'Many of you have used words like non-vegetarian and violent to describe Muslims. So you assume that the opposite is true for Hindus, that they are largely peace-loving and vegetarian. Go find out if that is true. See if you can find the answer to the question of whether most Hindus are vegetarian or not,' he said. The math was as telling as it was shocking. It turned out that 70 per cent of all Indians were non-vegetarian. If Pranav subtracted the Muslim population from this—14 per cent—it still left a fat chunk of 56 per cent that were meat-eaters. If this assumption about the difference between Hindus and Muslims didn't hold up, what about all the others he had been brought up with? Where had they come from, and why had no one done the math with him before?

With time, Pranav would deduce that his presumption about Hindus being largely vegetarian came from being surrounded mostly by upper castes who, in Gujarat, tended to be vegetarian. But even back then, it was apparent that there may be something seriously wrong with his presumptions about Hindus and Muslims. 'I was thinking about the connection I had often made between non-violence and vegetarianism. And how most of the participants in the violence of 2002 had been god-fearing and vegetarian. So something had gone terribly wrong, I knew that. And I told myself that if I wanted to figure it out, I would have to really keep an open mind.'

It was the hardest thing to contend with—the possibility that he had grown up with prejudice. Rejecting those ideas was like striking out against his childhood, his parents, the ground he stood on. On the other hand, he needed clarity.

'There was no way I could continue doing this work with the beliefs I had. I would either have to give up the job or find a way out.'

SIXTEEN

For Dungar, the torment was entirely physical. He was sent to prison on charges of burning down the houses of Muslims. The police registered a case in March 2002, and he was on the run for the next five months. Tending to his fields during the day and disappearing into the forest at night. It was summer and the heat was oppressive. But the cool grass underfoot and the warm wind overhead dulled his senses, so he managed to get some sleep. It was the uncertainty that got to Dungar. Not knowing if or when the chase would end.

A few months later, July arrived and, with it, the monsoon. The incessant rain made it impossible to sleep out in the open, with the infernal din of insects, the constant itching from bites and a forest floor squelchy with slush. Dungar sensed that his time was up. The police first caught up with his friend and partner in crime, Roop Sinh. They used him as bait to get to Dungar and the others. They said they would hold Sinh in jail without framing charges until all those named, including Dungar, surrendered to the police. Dungar knew it was only a matter of time before the police tracked him down. So he gave himself up in August, in deference to the inclement weather and persistent police.

'The first twenty-four hours in the lock up were terrible for me,' Dungar recalled. 'It was a tiny cell. There was no fan and there were so many mosquitoes.' The next day, he was shifted to the district jail. It was a large compound, and Dungar used his privileged position as a member of the Sangh Parivar to his advantage. He was allowed to spend his time on the lawns outside the jail cell, where he could walk freely, unlike the rest. 'Food would be sent for me from home. And I was allowed into the compound for twelve hours a day,' Dungar said, looking pleased. 'The six or seven others in my cell—all from my village, accused of the same crime—began to protest. They said to the jailer, how can you let him out and not the rest of us. I knew people, na.' In the evenings, he would settle down to a game of cards with some of the inmates. But at night he tossed and turned. How long would he remain in prison?

'I was filled with so much regret during those days in jail. I told myself that never again would I lift a finger against anyone. Even if I am beaten up, I will take it in my stride and not respond in kind. Not ever again,' he said. 'Those thirteen days felt like thirteen years.'

Fortunately for him, the VHP that he had so carefully cultivated delivered on its promise of protection. They sent to his rescue a lawyer who got him bail. Relieved as he was to be out of jail, Dungar still had to fight a case in court to have the charges against him dropped permanently. That was a much longer battle, and the outcome was far less certain. So Dungar decided not to count on the court alone for relief. Growing up, he had seen enough of the system to know that most manoeuvrings in the country took place outside officially mandated spaces. He came up with a more bankable plan. Threatening the witnesses one at a time.

The first to be silenced was Haji Parvez with the blue-and-white house that had burned for seven days.

Dungar glared at Parvez as he crossed him on the way to

court and said, 'You better have this case sorted out if you
ever want to set foot in that village again.'

Parvez had replied, 'I didn't give your name to the cops,'
his voice barely audible above the peon shouting out the
names of those due in court next.

'Well, whatever it is, it has to change if you want to
return home,' Dungar repeated.

At home, Dungar's father came out strongly in his
support. He did rounds of the village in his crumpled kurta
and dhoti, threatening Muslims with dire consequences if
they didn't drop their charges against his son. Sohail bhai*
the grocer, who lived across the street, was so scared that
he visited Dungar in jail, and even took his wife and kids
along to plead with him. When it was his turn to testify in
court, he said, 'I have no idea who burned down my house
and shop.' One by one, the Muslims dropped their charges.
All except Mohammad Asghar,* who refused to take his case
back. Asghar pointed straight at Dungar in court and said,
'Yes, this is the man who burned down my shop.'

His testimony ricocheted in the village. The Muslims that
were trying to return home wanted Asghar to drop his case.
Dungar was a powerful man, they said, and he was paving
the way for them to get back. Why was Asghar ruining their
chances? Some accused him of not caring because he didn't
live there. He only ran a shop in the area by day, and lived
some distance away in a village dominated by Muslims.
He could fight back because he had much less to lose, they
pointed out. For the sake of the rest, could he please relent?

Asghar refused. He had something to bargain with, and
he wanted that to be clear to Dungar. 'He set my shop on
fire. Let him rebuild it. Then I'll think about dropping the
charges,' he said.

Dungar's plan to intimidate his victims was coming unstuck. Even worse, the VHP-appointed lawyer was beginning to go back on his word. After appearing pro bono a few times, he began to ask for a big fat fee. Now it was beginning to hit home—the consequences of acting out on 28 February. Dungar was very worried. What if the case fell apart? He had worked so hard to rise above a life of drudgery, only to have it all come undone because of one frenzied moment when he had acted on provocation by the Sangh. He was angry with himself and the whole Hindu establishment. But a remarkably lucky break came from the unlikeliest place—an NGO.

A civil rights group was looking to partner with tribals in the area, and they stumbled upon Dungar. The regional head of the NGO was informed by his staff that Dungar had a tribal organisation of his own, and it already had a thousand members. 'That's good,' he told his team. 'We should capitalise on that.' When they first met, Dungar was hard at work in his shop. Corn cobs went in at one end of a large steel funnel and were tossed around till their spuds spilled out into a receptacle. Then the yellow buttons were crushed into a flaky white powder by a thick metal wheel. A large rat-a-tat sound filled the tiny room as corn sputtered across the mud floor. Dungar was a ghost caked in white dust when a skinny man walked in.

'Where can I find Dungar?' he inquired.

'What do you want?' Dungar responded, not knowing what to expect. 'He isn't here right now.'

'Nothing. Just tell him we'd like to meet him. We've heard he has an organisation that works with tribals.'

Now he was interested. 'I am Dungar,' he replied, black eyes gleaming from a powdery face.

'Well why didn't you say so in the first place?' the man from the NGO replied, slightly put off. But Dungar's broad grin was disarming. Besides, his reputation preceded him. So the stranger said, 'We run a programme for young people and we might be interested in partnering with your organisation.'

To start with, Dungar was wary. Years of VHP propaganda appeared before him like large statutory warnings. They had told tribals to stay away from the seductive charms of NGOs, that they were mostly Christian evangelists in disguise. What if they tried to turn him into a Christian? Dungar went back and forth with the NGO on this. Eventually, they managed to allay his fears by making him an offer he couldn't refuse. They had done their homework, and were aware of his crimes, the burning down of Muslim houses and the impending court case. 'They came to me with a proposal,' Dungar said. 'They asked me straight—tell us, whose houses did you burn down?' If he wanted to work with them, he would have to rebuild the homes of all the Muslims in the area. The money and material would be supplied by them. The on-site supervision would have to be his. It was a masterstroke. The NGO would use Dungar's existing network to grow tribal roots, and Dungar would be able to wipe clean his blemished record. It was as if the solution to his problem had materialised out of nowhere. He agreed to work with the NGO, and they agreed to deploy their lawyer to his case. 'I was scared,' Dungar said. 'Of Asghar and what he might do. So I said okay, yes, chalo!'

What began as a purely tactical arrangement, ended up affecting Dungar much more than he anticipated.

The NGO took him to meet the people he had displaced. 'That was the first time I truly understood that what I had done to the Muslims was terrible. Twelve families were displaced and homeless because of me,' he said. His own fear was now mixed with remorse. It was raining, and he saw the shaky shelter Sohailbhai was living in. 'He had built a makeshift shelter for himself and his family, and they slept on a bed stitched together with dried leaves. Most nights, they slept on empty stomachs. I came back home and wept continuously for forty minutes. When Sohailbhai saw me, he also cried. He said he didn't have anything to eat,' Dungar recalled. 'I sent him sacks of grain from my flour mill. Corn to make makkai rotlas for the next few months, until his house and shop could be rebuilt,' he explained. Dungar was now determined to bring back the Muslims he had displaced from the village.

But for that to happen, the environment of hostility he had helped create needed to be undone. Dungar held a meeting with the village headman and other powerful Hindus in the area. He needed to convince them that it would be a good thing if the Muslims returned. 'Look, with Sohailbhai's shop being shut, all of us have to travel ten kilometres just to buy half a kilo of cooking oil or dal. Why should we spend so much money going up and down for nothing? If his shop reopens, we will all save some,' Dungar said. Everyone could relate to the idea of saving money.

The village agreed to his proposition and construction began. The positioning was perfect for Dungar. He was seen standing at the work site, supervising labour, cement, supplies and the overall rebuilding of homes. But by now, there was more to it than that. It allowed him to sleep better. Things were looking up once again, and he was certain that the charges against him would soon be dropped, when the unexpected happened. The NGO lawyer who was fighting his case quit, and Dungar was left stranded, looking desperately for a replacement. This time, it was the VHP that came to the rescue.

Now Dungar was stuck between two opposing forces, and he was in no position to choose. So he didn't. He tried his best to keep both sides happy.

He hosted the NGO at home. They held a big meeting in the village. Several of its members were non-vegetarian, so Dungar had chicken brought in. It was cooked on a woodfire outside his house, so that his domestic kitchen would not be polluted by meat. At the same time, the NGO bosses would also be satisfied.

Alongside, he also attended VHP meetings. A very large show of solidarity was called for in the town of Godhra. This was the town where the train had been burnt. On the appointed day, the place was packed with VHP leaders and volunteers from all over Gujarat. The unwritten code for all those present was to brag about what they had done to Muslims in their region. 'I set their homes on fire,' Dungar bragged, even as he set the wheels in motion to undo the act. The bragging got him a new lawyer, who fought his case until the charges against him were eventually dropped.

SEVENTEEN

In Chharanagar, the air was still toxic after the violence of the mob. But once the hate had spent itself, what followed was fear. The fear of being caught by the police. The violence Suresh had meted out as a key member of the mob now had a label. It was described by the papers and TV channels as 'the Naroda Patiya case', the site where the worst crimes against Muslims had taken place. What put it in the spotlight was the fact that the dots from that massacre were being joined to the political party in power, the BJP. Many people had started to say that they had seen people from the party instigating the mob. One person in particular featured constantly in testimonies to the police and civil society groups—a prominent party leader and a member of the state assembly called Maya Kodnani. She was a gynaecologist from the wealthy Sindhi community. She had short hair and a strong jaw, and practised in the area. Most people recognised her. Maya was also a long-serving BJP leader who had won two elections from the area.

Witnesses described how the mob that had gathered around the Noorani Masjid in Naroda Patiya was a small tangle of people throwing stones at each other before Maya arrived in her white Maruti car. It was only after she gesticulated to a retreating mob that things took a dramatic turn, they said. The mob did an about turn, went on the offensive and started to grow exponentially.

Maya Kodnani had delivered babies and attended to pregnant couples from Chharanagar and Naroda Patiya, so people like Abdul Majid, who lost nine members of his family, recognised her. Just as he recognised Suresh, whom he had seen even as a child. Majid had taken his pregnant wife to the doctor-politician a few years before 2002, and he claimed that she had read the ultrasound all wrong. She had told Majid he would have a girl, but it turned out to be a boy. Years later, inchoate as he recounted the events of that time, Majid said he knew there was something wrong with the doctor. She couldn't even read an ultrasound. The boy she delivered was his youngest, Khwaja Hussain. He was one of the nine from Majid's family who was killed by the mob in 2002, at the age of five. Majid found Hussain's body two days later, his small hand still gripping a knife. He had fought bravely, Majid was told by those who saw him die. 'I'll get you, you bastards!' he had shouted.

No one could possibly ease Majid's torment. Or make him un-see Suresh and Mayaben. As news of possible links to top leaders kept the story in the headlines, Suresh knew he would be arrested. So he did what he had always done when the police was after him. He fled to his cousin's house in a village some distance away, expecting to return once the heat died down. This time, however, it wasn't dying down. The police turned up at his door and would not go away. Not even at 3 a.m., when they continued to stalk Farzana, hoping it would eventually get Suresh to return. When that didn't work, the local cop struck a deal with Suresh's chacha, Jayantibhai. 'Just ask him to give himself up, we'll let him go in a few days, pucca.' The chacha's appeal finally brought Suresh back home at four in the afternoon. He was immediately whisked away by the police.

Soon, it became clear to Suresh and the forty-five others who were arrested, why the police was zealously pursuing them. To deflect the sting of accusations from the state and the BJP. But those accusatory fingers did not go away, especially when the arrests were seen to be selective. It seemed to those tracking the case that Suresh was dispensable to the Sangh Parivar but Maya Kodnani was not. Despite several eyewitness accounts, Maya was not arrested until five years later. In that time, she had contested and won another election on a BJP ticket, and was even made minister for Women and Child Welfare. If Mayaben wasn't going to be arrested, then others in the mob would have to be held to account. It was slowly dawning on Suresh that the charges against him were not going to come unstuck so easily. He should never have listened to his chacha and allowed the police to arrest him.

Fifteen days later, when Jayantibhai and Farzana were allowed to visit him in Sabarmati jail, he lashed out: 'You motherfucker! Look at what you made me do! I'll be in jail forever. Now go on, go home and fuck my wife!'

His uncle spat back, 'How was I supposed to know what you've been doing? Tell me that. How come my name isn't with the police? Because I didn't do anything!'

In the middle of this volatility, Farzana needed to process her own feelings. It was clear to her that this was not like the past arrests. This was going to be the long haul, and she and their two small children would get the worst of it. 'Why did you have to do this? What am I supposed to do now?' she turned despairingly to Suresh, feeling completely abandoned. But he was in no mood to be held to account by anyone, least of all his wife. How dare she ask questions. 'Go marry someone else, you cunt,' he replied.

Nothing made sense to Farzana. Everything was a blur.

Looking back, it was difficult to figure out the exact sequence of events. Had there been a heated exchange when she met Suresh in jail, or was that only a figment of her imagination? It would have been far easier if Suresh was just one thing to her. A husband that she could paint black, and dismiss out of hand, a predictable set of emotions in play. But it wasn't like that. The memory of the day she saw him in jail was messy, like her feelings for Suresh were. Just when she thought she had captured it, another version appeared before her. In this, Suresh was softer, more vulnerable, and as much of a mess as she was. When they met, he was also in tears. She broke down, then he did.

'Don't worry please,' Suresh pleaded with her. 'I will get out of here soon. You just focus on looking after our kids, okay? And don't step out. It's not safe for you. Don't go anywhere. Just stay home and take care of yourself.'

Farzana was hysterical. 'What has my life become? You are in jail. What am I supposed to do with our two kids?'

Suresh tried to reassure her, 'There's always my aunt and uncle. Don't worry about that. They will provide for all of you, and look after you till I get out.'

What was the real story, where was the real Suresh? There were always two versions competing for space in her head. One dominated by violence, the other by love. In fact, the two were possibly the same, the space where all of Suresh's responses came from. A space of torment.

EIGHTEEN

The torment that Pranav's job caused him was slow, insidious. Working with Muslims every single day exposed him not only to the devastation of the twenty-eighth but also to their culture, religion and eating habits. It started to change him in ways he could not understand. Like the fervour with which he ate mutton, as if it were replacement for religion, although he had been raised a vegetarian. Bhuna gosht. Succulent pieces of goat meat cooked in browned onions with a sprinkling of coriander powder and some bay leaves to complement the spices. Sweet-smelling cardamom and cinnamon sticks added next, and stirred into an intoxicating curry. It filled an inexplicable void in a life full of paradoxes. Why was something new and alien more comforting than the old familiar?

It certainly dulled the pain and guilt he felt every time he heard a story of what the mobs had done. The proximity to his new fraternity hurt most in the evenings, which was when Pranav met his old friends. His former hostel-mates, who were like a second family. These were the people he had wanted to build his life around. It was his attachment to them that had made him take up the NGO job in the first place. He had wanted to be in the same university town that they all lived in. Now, when he met them after work, he realised how much he was changing—the things he wanted to share with them most were things he had to hide.

But even worse than the loneliness and alienation was the nagging feeling Pranav had when he tried to sleep at night. 'I asked myself why I did not have the same response to help the victims of the 2002 violence the way I had pitched in for survivors of the 2001 earthquake. It made me feel very guilty when I thought about it.'

Now, when he needed someone to talk to more than ever, there was no one around. Luckily for Pranav, his work had become all-consuming. His boss sent him to take charge of work in another district for a month while the woman in charge there went on leave. This was a part of Gujarat that had seen some of the worst violence in 2002. It was where his NGO was involved in a large relief-and-rehabilitation project. He arrived on a November afternoon to find his colleague impatient to leave. 'I went in and she started with the handover immediately, tak-tak-tak,' Pranav said. 'This is the number of the contractor in charge of the construction work, here's the guy in charge of the relief camp, here's the person who knows the victims. Okay, now can I go?' she turned to Pranav and asked. In two hours, she had finished handing over and left.

Pranav noticed that there was another trainee-staffer in the office, just like him. An agreeable-looking young man called Vikram.*

'Do you know where we can grab a bite?' Pranav asked him.

'No, man, I also just got here.'

Pranav discovered that his new friend was from the south of India, and on an internship from his college. 'Let's go see where we can get something to eat,' he suggested, and the two of them set out on their bikes. When they returned, there were four people waiting outside the office.

'Pranavbhai,' one of them said when he ushered them in, 'get me also on board as a sub-contractor, na. I'll pay you whatever you want on the side.' This was a strange, shifty-eyed man.

Pranav was aghast. 'That is not how things work here,' he said, his temper rising.

'Of course it is,' the man replied. 'It's all set here, there are fixed rates for everyone.'

Pranav dismissed everyone, dialled his boss and told him what he had stumbled upon. A well-oiled system of bribes. 'You deal with it however you like,' said the boss, while also making it clear that corruption would not be tolerated. Pranav called the chief contractor—a powerful Muslim leader from the area, Javedbhai.*

'Let's have a meeting with all the sub-contractors,' Pranav said to him. 'Will you call them all, please—the brick supplier, cement-wala?'

Everyone turned up at 9 p.m. as instructed. Pranav was a man on a mission. 'All of you, just tell me what your outstanding dues are. What we owe you,' he said. Everyone raised bills as asked, not knowing what was coming next. Once the bills were collected and dues settled, he looked up at all the sub-contractors gathered in the tiny office and declared, 'None of you will supply material anymore. From this day on, all your contracts are terminated.'

The contractors were shocked. 'What, why?' they asked, trying to make sense of what had just happened.

There was no answer. Pranav was cold as ice. The axe had come down hard, and the contractors were irate and indignant.

They complained to Pranav's colleague who was on leave. She, in turn, called him. 'What the hell are you doing?' she yelled into the phone. Pranav replied coolly, 'I haven't done anything. I am merely following the boss's instructions. If you have a problem with that, take it up with him directly. Or better still, cancel your holiday and come back.' Having delivered his dare, Pranav went about setting up an entirely new system.

Payments would be made out in cheques, not cash. When the construction material was delivered, a receipt would need to be signed by three people from the village. After the summary dismissal of the old contractors, Pranav and Vikram set out in search of new ones. He was exhilarated to discover this side to himself—the hyper-organised man in charge. But it was also confusing. He had only just warmed to the plight of Muslim victims, and now had to confront the reality that people didn't operate in neat little boxes. All Muslims were not victims. There were also a few corrupt, conniving Islamist leaders grabbing every contract they could. He was trying to get rid of his prejudice, and people like these were making it impossible.

'What bastards they are, eating into their own community's relief fund,' Pranav said to his boss over the phone, in a state of distress. 'How can they do that?'

His boss calmed him down. 'You have to understand the victim's psychology,' he said.

'But those contractors are not victims!' Pranav shot back.

His boss tried to explain. 'You are only looking literally at the victims of violence. But, in fact, the whole community of Muslims in India are victims of deep-rooted prejudice. So, many of them tend to grab what they get when they can.'

Pranav was unconvinced. Why was everything so complicated? He knew in his head that he wanted to fight for these people. But he was fighting for people he didn't fully understand. This was not how it was supposed to be.

At the next training that the NGO conducted, Pranav made a list of things he wanted to change about himself. He wrote right on top, 'I want to change the way I think about Muslims.' It was the most difficult thing to admit, even to himself. Much later, he described it thus: 'When your head has been stuffed with so much propaganda, you are also as good as a victim.' Pranav was entirely unaware of the fact that his 'victimhood' was precisely why he had been hired in the first place. It was part of the NGO's design. They calculated that if the environment of hostility in Gujarat was to change, it had to happen by including both Muslims and Hindus in the post-violence reconstruction. Both were victims of circumstance and propaganda, both had baggage to shed. This was why one of the preconditions during the recruitment drive was to get Muslims and Hindus to form teams and come up with project proposals together. That precondition was what had brought Pranav on board with his friend Tanveer. Yet, no one had accounted for the profound unravelling that Pranav would go through.

It shattered him, his boss said, adding that this was very rare. 'There were others who were recruited for the same reason as Pranav,' he said, scratching his chin and peering over his glasses. 'But they left.' And that was where Pranav stood out. Despite the frightening mutation, he had the integrity and curiosity to power on. 'Remember, at twenty-one or twenty-two, you're not really an adult. There is huge parental pressure. And the moment the new recruits told their parents they had worked in relief camps, I mean, it was finished. So, the fact that he withstood the peer pressure was rare.' The man beamed. 'He had strong peer pressure I think; given where he went to college, I can understand, because it's a hardcore anti-Muslim space.'

Pranav's boss had got that exactly right. Among his buddies from college, this new job was trivia to be tossed around in jest. His arched eyebrows and trademark disdain that had once made him their gang leader were now scoffed at as the bluster of a friend gone rogue. 'Pranav needs to stop this stuff he's saying and doing. I will convert him back,' said his former classmate. At these times, it didn't help that, even in his own head, Pranav wasn't sure of his motivations. The old idea he had of himself—who he was, what he believed in—was fading. And the new one was still in an embryonic state, full of discomfiting thoughts and ideological positions he wasn't always sure how to hold. He was lost.

One day, in the middle of an intense workshop, Pranav had a breakdown. 'He cried when he started to talk about who he was before,' his boss recalled, pausing to let that sink in and then saying emphatically, 'And he does not break down often, uhh … He breaks down when he's very angry. Or when it has hit him very hard. Otherwise he's very masculine. Unlike me, for example—I'll start crying at every … errr …' he trailed off, welling up at the picture of Pranav he was describing.

The real question for his boss was this: how much would Pranav be able to take, and for how long? He felt it could go either way. Stepping into this new world meant acknowledging that almost everything he had grown up with was wrong. And Pranav had come too far to go back. For a while, he coped by outsourcing all the self-loathing to his family. It was their fault for bringing him up the way they had—'I admit I tried to transfer that hate,' he said.

While he was tormented and robbed of his sleep, his boss decided that it was time to throw the young man into the deep end. He was transferred from the university town to the regional office where he had already spent a month, ridding the place of corruption. It was also a place that had been the fulcrum of hate and violence in 2002. The relocation forced Pranav into a crisis he had been studiously avoiding—having to wrestle with himself and who he had been until this time. So far, he had avoided dealing directly with the victims, or hearing their stories first-hand. But his new office was tasked with handling the case of a woman who had been gangraped and left for dead under a pile of her relatives' bodies. She had survived, and was determined to tell her story. Pranav's office was helping her access the police and courts, so he was forced to listen to her.

'I did not cry at the time,' he said, looking away. 'I was speechless. I kept thinking to myself—kya hua, why did this happen?' After hearing her story, everything changed for him. 'I decided I was going to work in this space for the rest of my life.' He was aware by now that the shedding of old baggage wasn't the freeing, lightening of load it was often mistakenly described as. It would leave permanent scars and be a formidable load to bear. He described the heaviness: 'There is your family and the friends you had or still have ... That is a completely different space. I would try not to talk about my work, but then, how long can you stay silent? Suddenly something will erupt from your side also.'

As Pranav changed, more and more people from his former life began to feel disconnected from him. 'Oh, he's no good anymore.'

From rushing back to the university town to meet his friends every weekend, Pranav now went one weekend a month, then less and less. And home? He hardly ever went home.

NINETEEN

With Suresh in jail, Farzana felt the gullies of Chharanagar closing in on her. She was not just Farzana, she was 'that Musalmaan'. The word curled around the tongues of Suresh's family. It was calculated to impress upon Farzana her place in the world, so she would crawl with fear, lurk in quiet corners and keep her head down. Since she had cut herself off from her family six years ago, Farzana had to put up with it. It only took half an hour in an autorickshaw to get from Chharanagar to Jamalpur, but her parents' home may as well have been on Mars. If it was impossible for them to meet before 2002, afterwards, it was like asking to be killed. As soon as images of the violence flashed on TVs across the city, Khatoonbibi assumed that her daughter was dead. There was no way to check. Neither she nor Farzana had cellphones at the time. The only way to get in touch was by calling Suresh's chachi, which at the time seemed impossible. It was easier to assume she was dead than live with the uncertainty.

Many months went by. When the violence abated, there was a wedding in Naroda Patiya, and Farzana's relatives were invited. Now her mother could not contain herself. She asked two of the kids at the wedding to go across to the other side, and find out if Farzana still lived there. Two girls in shiny wedding clothes made their way to Radhaben's house. She guessed they were from Farzana's home. 'Yes, she does live here, but she has also gone out to attend a wedding in the area,' Radha informed them. Her mother couldn't believe what she heard. Her daughter was alive. Within the next few days, she plucked up the courage to call Radhaben and ask to speak with Farzana.

Radhaben handed Farzana the phone. 'It's your mother.'

Farzana choked when she heard her mother's voice. 'Now you found time to call me, after all this?' she said between big, hysterical sobs.

Her mother had a long list of questions. 'Why didn't you come and see me after you had the kids? Why didn't you bring my grandchildren to me?' she demanded to know, also breaking down at the other end.

'With what face would I come home to you, Ammi? I didn't want to be a burden,' Farzana said.

The atmosphere of fear being what it was, even after the long cathartic phone call, they did not dare meet.

With Suresh in jail, Farzana's primary concern was survival. In the first few weeks, his chacha–chachi lived up to their promise of looking out for her and the two children. They gave her a monthly allowance for basics—dal, roti and subzi. School fees weren't an issue since their daughter Richie went to a government school where no fee was charged, and their boy Vivian wasn't enrolled in school at the time. But it wasn't enough. Over time, Farzana needed to find ways to make some money. 'I used to rent out our electricity,' she admitted. They had an official electricity meter, and for Rs 200–300 per person, she sublet her connection. Farzana also washed dishes and clothes in people's homes. She was paid Rs 20 for the clothes and another twenty for the dishes, which added up to a total of Rs 40 per home per day. Some people also gave her leftovers to eat. Despite all of this, the debts started to pile up. Creditors arrived at the door, threatening to have her and the kids evicted if dues weren't paid. When Farzana reported this to Suresh in jail, he said, 'Just get me some parole time, and I will take care of it.' But that meant finding still more money to grease the right palms to get him out. Suresh would have to say he was ill and needed treatment to be granted leave. She would need to get a fake medical certificate to produce along with his application. And that is when Farzana decided to try her hand at the family trade—thieving.

She asked a group of Chhara women thieves if she could go along with them on their next gig. 'Are you sure you're up for this?' they asked her, surprised. 'Yes, yes, I'll do the best I can, whatever you say,' Farzana pleaded. They agreed. She was to play the decoy in their next act. Farzana was instructed to stand at the vegetable seller's cart and distract the woman buyer they had zeroed in on, so that the others could steal her purse. She delivered on her task, and the heist was successful. After the proceeds were divided up, Farzana's share amounted to Rs 75. She was relieved to have made some money. But as soon as she got home, Suresh's chachi summoned her.

'You will not go out thieving again,' Radhaben said sternly. 'Those are the worst sort of people to hang out with, and I don't want you mingling with them.' There was a pecking order amongst the thieves of Chharanagar. Radha had stopped going out, but in her heyday, she was the proud thief of the jewellery market. It was highbrow work compared with the lowly snatching of purses. Farzana nodded obediently, and looked for more domestic chores to tend to in people's homes. Meanwhile, Radhaben threw in a warning or two to make sure Farzana knew her place. 'Don't go around interacting with your kind of people and spreading canards about your husband,' she threatened.

What complicated everything was the affection for Suresh that Farzana thought she was done with but discovered she was not. She saw how, despite himself, he was also in love with her. Suresh had found extraordinary ways to demonstrate this while he was in jail. There was an inmate he found who could sketch and paint. He instructed, and possibly threatened, him to sketch scenes from his life with his family. When Farzana met him in jail, he presented her with many such drawings. Of her crying when she came to visit him. Of her holding the baby Vivian. Of Richie. And then he looked at her from behind the prison bars and said, 'I really love you a whole lot.'

Like the forty-five others accused in the Naroda Patiya case, Suresh got bail in October 2002. But not long after, he was back in prison. This time in the city of Vadodara, for four years, on charges of theft and looting. Suresh and one of his uncles had just looted a shop that traded in gold—a particularly profitable heist—but got caught while they were returning home. Farzana was beginning to accept the fact that she would have to earn their keep and raise the two children by herself. The effort was punishing, but it also made her more assertive. On one of the brief interludes when Suresh was out on parole and his pent-up rage in full force, she plucked up the courage to talk back. 'You Musalmaani. I only married you for revenge,' he said to her. And she shot back, 'Well, now you've married me, so behave like my husband.'

Her assertiveness and his need to crush her became the double helix of their relationship. One day, it involved a knife. Suresh used it to gouge flesh out of his wife's shoulder. Farzana went blank with pain and left the house bleeding, with one thought only: she had to make it to Jamalpur, to her mother's house. She just had to. She fainted.

Khatoonbibi was at home when a neighbour came running to say breathlessly, 'Come quickly, it's your daughter.' Farzana had fainted from the loss of blood. And since she was returning to Jamalpur after so many years, she had forgotten the way back home and had ended up in the next lane. 'When I went to fetch her, I was struck by the fact that the girl sitting there didn't even look like my daughter. Her face was unrecognisable,' Khatoonbibi recalled, sobbing at the memory of it. 'Her clothes were torn, her shoulder was torn, her body was covered with black bruises. And she was stooping over, unable to stand straight.' They both sat and wept, mother and daughter. Khatoonbibi took Farzana to the doctor. She fed her, bathed her, tended to her constantly. The very next day, a repentant Suresh turned up at their door. 'Please forgive me, Ammi,' he wailed loudly, touching his mother-in-law's feet. He heaped on entreaties of love and spoke of how he could not bear to be without his wife for a single moment. When that didn't seem to work, he changed tack. He tried to reason with her by saying that he was in jail. His life was over. Everything that was his was now Farzana's. Besides, the kids missed her.

Khatoonbibi relented. 'Look, he says he can't live without you,' she repeated to Farzana. 'Go back to him.'

The truth of the matter was that her parents could not keep her at home—Suresh's menacing presence would be an inescapable consequence of it. Everyone knew of his role in the Naroda Patiya violence. And in the Muslim-majority ghetto they lived in, having one of the main actors in that massacre turn up at their door endangered everyone. Farzana went back.

Khatoonbibi decided to play peacemaker, especially after she saw the state her daughter was in. She called her daughter on Suresh's aunt's phone, and invited the two of them home for a meal.

'Ammi has called us home,' Farzana said to Suresh.

'I don't eat at the house of a Musalmaan,' was his instant reply. 'They are calling me to have me killed,' he added viciously. And then he conceded. They would go, he declared to her, but only on the condition that she dressed as a Hindu wife. 'You will not wear this Punjabi dress,' he said, referring to her salwar kameezes. 'You will go dressed in a sari with red sindoor on your forehead and a tikka.'

They went to Jamalpur for lunch. Khatoonbibi had cooked up a storm. But Suresh ate sparingly and made sure the visit was as short as possible. When they returned home, Farzana overheard him tell his uncle and aunt, 'The next time her mother calls on your phone, don't answer. Or just say it's the wrong number.'

By now, Suresh was hitting out not just at Farzana but at anyone and everyone on his radar, including his uncle. He fought with Jayantibhai over the proceeds of a round of successful thieving. This time, it was Suresh who took a massive beating. His uncle broke several bones in his body. The most damage was to his left leg—his already weak polio-leg. It was shattered so badly that it took five people to lift him out of his bed for the next two years. Farzana remembered those days of being by his side every waking moment. 'I used to help him shit and piss. He couldn't even do that without help from me,' she said.

It was on one of those days, in the summer of 2007, when Suresh's leg was starting to heal but he was still bed-ridden, that a young bearded stranger stopped by.

He said he was from the VHP, and was collecting stories of Hindu evangelists defending their faith. After a long listless phase, suddenly there was a spark in Suresh. He asked the visitor to sit down and instructed Farzana to carry him to a clearing outside the house, where the men could talk in peace. And then he bragged about what he had done in 2002.

Suresh was animated. 'We'd finished burning everything and had returned,' he said, gesticulating with his arms. 'That was when the police called us ... They said some Muslims were hiding in this sewer ... When we went there, we saw their houses had been completely burned down, but seven or eight of them had hidden in the gutter ... We shut the lid on it ... If we'd gone in after them, we might have been in danger ... We closed the lid and weighted it down with big boulders ... Later, they found eight or ten corpses in there ... They'd gone there to save their lives, but ... they died of the gases down there ... This happened in the evening ... the *dhamal* [killing spree] went [on] till night, till about 8.30.'†

Now he was on a roll. The man egged him on. 'So you went in again?'

'We were inside ... By evening, things had cooled down ... We were tired also ... After all, a man gets tired out ... Hurling stones, beating with pipes, stabbing, all this ...'

Suresh spoke animatedly as his listener nodded in agreement.

'The way we came out from inside could only be done by a man of strong heart.'

---

† From *Tehelka* magazine's published transcripts, 12 August 2007. The entire conversation reproduced here is from this source.

And then he talked about seeing the BJP gynaecologist–politician Maya Kodnani moving around in an open jeep.

'She kept raising slogans ... She said, carry on with your work, I'm here [to protect you] ... She was wearing a white sari and had on a saffron band ... I had also tied on a saffron band ...'

Suresh had absolutely no idea that, with every line he spoke, he was incriminating himself before a man who was only posing as a member of the VHP, but was in fact Ashish Khetan, the investigations head at the news magazine *Tehelka*. What he said next would end up being used as very strong corroborative evidence in a court case that would eventually convict him. The sting video was made public in August that year. While speaking to Suresh, Khetan had a tiny camera pinned to his shirt lapel, concealed in the buttonhole. It was the size of a large fly. In sharp contrast to the portrait Farzana had painted of Suresh as being uncommunicative, talking only in monosyllables, here he was, letting loose a verbal torrent.

'Batteries were burning ... gas cylinders were burning ... Some pigs were sleeping under a truck ... We killed a pig, four or five of us Chharas got together and killed the pig ... Then we hung the pig up from the mosque and raised a saffron flag ... Eight or 10 of us climbed on top ... We tried hard but the masjid didn't break ...'

Ashish Khetan pressed on, and said to Suresh, 'It is being said the Chharas also committed rapes.'

Suresh had reached a point of no return.

'Now look, one thing is true ... *bhookhe ghuse to koi na koi to phal khayega, na* [when thousands of hungry men go in, they will eat some fruit or the other, no] ... *Aise bhi, phal ko kuchal ke phenk denge* [in any case, the fruit was going to be crushed and thrown away] ... Look, I'm not telling lies ... Mata is before me [*gesturing to an image of a deity*] ... Many Muslim girls were being killed and burnt to death anyway, some people must have helped themselves to the fruit ...

'... The more you harm them, the less it is ... I really hate them ... don't want to spare them ... Look, my wife is sitting here but let me say ... the fruit was there so it had to be eaten ... I also ate ... I also ate ... I ate once.'

Ashish insisted, 'Just once?'

Suresh replied, 'Just once ... then I had to go killing again ... [*turns to relative Prakash Rathod and talks about the girl he had raped and killed*] ... That scrap-dealer's girl, Naseemo ... Naseemo, that juicy plump one ... I got on top.'

Ashish remarked, 'She didn't survive, did she?'

'No,' said Suresh. And added, 'Then I pulped her ... Made her into a pickle.'

Farzana could no longer pretend that she did not know what her husband had done. 'Why did you tell me you didn't do anything, haan?' Farzana asked Suresh later that night, still in a state of shock from what she had heard.

'Just shut up and mind your own business,' was Suresh's reply.

A few days later, Farzana ran back to her parents in Jamalpur. How could she continue to live with this man, she asked her mother. Their conversation was interrupted by a phone call from Suresh's aunt. 'Come back home please, this man has a broken leg. Who will take him to shit and piss?' Radhaben pleaded.

Farzana's mother agreed. 'Go back. What's done is done. If you ditch him in this time of distress, everyone will say you left him because of his bad leg,' she said. Besides, there were the two children to think about.

As soon as Farzana returned home, Suresh hit her with his caustic tongue. 'Turns out your mum finds it hard to feed you, haan? She didn't want to keep you or what?'

Farzana had nothing to say.

TWENTY

Dungar focused on bringing back the Muslims whose homes he had destroyed. For two years after 2002, he stood at the construction site and supervised the work on thirty-nine houses across the block of five villages. The first to move back home was Sohailbhai and his family after more than a year of being destitute. Next was Sheikh Suleiman,* who returned to his big old house, now repaired and rendered new. His family had lived in the village for three generations. Dungar's father and he had been in school together. Suleiman remembered the day he left. 'I fled the house with my younger son before it was attacked. It was all completely burnt. The timber roof was charred. So were the walls. Only the Quran remained untouched,' he said, overcome with emotion. The home had contained so much history and such a sense of belonging. When he was summoned in court later to testify in the case against Dungar, Suleiman swore on the Quran and said, 'I had gone away when the house was burned, so I don't know who did it.' Along with the houses, Dungar's image was being reconstructed as that of a repentant Hindu. As a man with some social standing and clout that a well-established NGO had backed.

But the new liberal patina didn't stick. Once the houses were built and the cases against him started to crumble, cracks appeared in Dungar's relationship with the NGO. Things came to a head over goat-rearing. The NGO saw that the Bhils, Rathwas and other communities in the village reared goats, and so did the Muslims. They decided to give all of these communities professional training in animal husbandry as a way of dialling down the post-2002 hostility. Veterinary services were activated. Goats from a superior stock were imported from neighbouring Rajasthan to improve the local gene pool. A common trading point was set up for Muslim traders and tribal herders to sort out their differences.

Dungar held a meeting for the NGO in his house. Key members from the head office came down from Ahmedabad, and more than a hundred people from the village attended.

The NGO decided to talk to Dungar about the trust he ran for tribal welfare that had a distinctly Sangh Parivar flavour and name. They told Dungar how that was a problem for them, and that he needed to fix it if he wanted their working relationship to continue. The idea that all tribals were Hindus, this would have to change, the NGO insisted. Dungar evaded the subject. 'Let's talk about that some other time. For now, should we just focus on the task at hand?'

But postponing the confrontation only made things worse. The NGO held a training programme at a large campsite on the outskirts of Ahmedabad. It was meant to inspire tribals to come forward and steer their own path, underline their own identity instead of obliterating it in favour of a homogenous Hindu hat. The politics were set sharply against the BJP–VHP–RSS even if it was not explicitly stated. But that is not how Dungar saw it. What he understood was that it would be good business and a great morale booster. Everyone in the village had seen him work with the NGO and trusted him. They were happy to be on board with anything that could improve their prospects in a village with a dead economy. Dungar told the NGO that he would attend their training session and bring a hundred people with him. This was exactly the kind of partnership the NGO was hoping for.

'It was meant to be a seven-day workshop,' Dungar recalled. 'We were all meant to attend the training programme and the meals were provided by them. But they served meat on the table along with vegetarian food.' He frowned. 'Most of the people I had brought with me were not comfortable eating at a table where meat was being served. So I suggested to the organisers that they make food separately for us in a vegetarian kitchen. Otherwise the same spoons and utensils may be used for the meat dishes and the vegetarian food. And that was a big problem.' And then came the final nail in the coffin. One of the participants from his village spotted a picture of Jesus Christ on the premises. They felt their worst fears had come true. This was a Christian evangelist organisation in disguise.

'I tried to explain to people that there was no such thing happening. But they wouldn't listen. They shouted back at me and said that I was also Christian. Dungar is Christian, he's working with a group of Christian converts, they started saying about me.' It was a big embarrassment for Dungar, who had counted on the event being a demonstration of his clout. Instead, it was beginning to snowball into a crisis that threatened to take his reputation down. He was at a crossroads, and he had to choose between offending the NGO or his village. Dungar chose to appease his people and dump the NGO.

To make sure the village got the messaging right and no one mistook him for a Christian evangelist, Dungar even joined a mob from the village when they ganged up against the NGO later that year. 'I was part of the group of about twenty-five people that surrounded them. We made them all run. We beat them all up,' he said happily. 'I didn't meet them for many years after that day.'

Now Dungar had only the VHP and the umbrella of the Sangh Parivar to fall back on. There was no looking back. It was 2005. The houses were built. The VHP had appointed a lawyer to fight Dungar's case. Seeing how popular he was in the area, they made him secretary for the entire block. It was a reward he had earned for his loyalty to the Parivar and for outdoing everyone in the tasks he was assigned. As his stature rose, the Sangh suggested that he contest the next election at the block level on a BJP party ticket.

'I had thought about it even when I was with the NGO, that once I pick up the ropes of how to work the system, I will enter politics,' Dungar said. A local election was a very big deal. More deals were done, schemes inked and power wielded at this level than higher up the hierarchy. Proximity to the voters and the direct bearing each vote would have on their election considerably upped the stakes. It was an intoxicating time. And Dungar knew exactly what was required. He had done it before, albeit on a smaller scale. He had fought and won a village council election when he was just eighteen years old.

'At that time, the whole village had asked me to stand for the panchayat elections. They said I would be a good candidate because of how agreeable I was and how I got on with everybody. I used to sing well at the bhajan-satsangs. That played a big part in my being noticed,' Dungar said. He used the kite as his election symbol, especially since elections were being held around the time of the big annual kite festival of Gujarat, Uttarayan. 'I had saved up 5,000 rupees from the construction work I did, and I used that to get the villagers drunk. I fed them meat and got them their alcohol fix, so I won that election comfortably,' Dungar said, smiling, nostrils flaring with remembered excitement.

It was good practice and astute politics. He had learnt young that elections in Gujarat were all about being Janus-faced. Posturing as a devout Hindu to enamour the electorate, and then doing the exact opposite to pull through. He bribed them with the only currency that was an absolute prerequisite to winning an election in a state where drinking was prohibited.

Now that he was contesting an election at the block level and on a BJP ticket, the stakes were much higher. But the BJP knew what they were doing. The constituency included a cluster of Muslim-majority villages, where Dungar had just finished rebuilding homes. The seat was reserved for a tribal candidate, so the BJP calculated that he was their best bet. 'I told people that I will work for the welfare of tribals and Hindus. And I also went to the Muslim bastis, to Muslim homes,' Dungar said. 'I had run sewing classes for the women there for two years when I was with the NGO.' That association had improved his standing considerably. It didn't matter that his relationship with the NGO had fallen apart. It helped him defeat a long-standing Congress party rival. He got 6,400 votes while his rival managed a measly 700. From volunteering with the Sangh in the 1990s to joining them in the year 2000 to winning an election five years later—it was a meteoric rise.

'People knew me across the entire block of five villages,' Dungar said. 'And they came to me to sort out many of their problems. I would call both sides, take the 200-rupee fee for resolving the dispute that was customary in the village. And I would spend it on getting both sides food and drink. They would get high, not me,' he said.

Dungar would sit back and watch. And think about how much his life had changed.

TWENTY-ONE

In the new world Pranav had chosen for himself, he was trying hard to figure out a way to be. He stared fixedly at his computer until 3 a.m. on most nights. He had been sent to his NGO's regional office to oversee some of the most challenging post-violence work. But it was hard. 'There was a lot of guilt associated with being a Hindu,' he said. 'I felt ki, who am I? Where am I and where am I going from here?' He couldn't bear to think about his old life and the ideas he had grown up with. He now saw how deeply they were connected with the destruction of Muslims. But it was also impossible to disregard where he came from.

'You cannot leave behind your community or your family. They will remain with you,' he explained. 'And there will always be some point at which you will say that you are different from the other side as well.' The side of the Muslims and the development sector in which he now worked. 'So this crisis will be there forever. You feel like you are not in the old place or the new. You're standing somewhere in the middle with no idea where you will go from here.'

He buried himself in work, and stayed up chatting with colleagues until late. When they went home, he invented more work. Writing reports until midnight, endless amounts of research, anything to avoid dealing with his central dilemma. 'Everything was off,' is how he later described his trauma.

'When I look back now, I can see that I tried to avoid getting into a conversation with myself. My emotional side was closed.'

But it could not go on like that forever. 'I slowly started realising that this was not okay,' he said. He reached out to his friend and colleague Vikram to try and make sense of the confusion in his head. But he was still too scared to admit the whole truth of his past. So he phrased his questions in vague generalities. Like asking Vikram to explain the distinction between religion and indoctrination. 'It was not ki I am feeling this, I am feeling that,' Pranav said, smiling. 'We talked about larger issues. Like about the RSS. I had no idea what the organisation was about, or its history. He was very well versed with all of this, because his parents were from the NGO sector. So, right from his childhood, he grew up with that exposure. And I learned many new things from him.' Pranav remembers their conversations vividly.

'He explained what saffronisation was. He gave the example of our schools and said, why was there only one kind of prayer being said? I could relate to that. In my school, that's exactly how it was. There would be a photo of Goddess Saraswati placed in front of us, and we would garland it and all. The prayers were all entirely Hindu. There was never a Muslim prayer, or a Christian one, or even a neutral one,' Pranav said.

Looking back fondly on those times, Vikram remembered one conversation in particular. 'I said that there is nothing wrong with being Hindu, but there is something wrong with taking that religion and making it an agenda for politics.' Pranav had listened quietly, hiding the fact that some of these ideas were new and revolutionary to him, and required enormous internal processing.

When things got too intense, he suggested to Vikram that they take off on their bikes, head out across the Gujarat border to the nearest liquor shop and get completely drunk. 'We went across the border to Madhya Pradesh,' Vikram recalled. 'And stopped for beer at the first place we found. It was terrible. I've never had worse beer in my life. It tasted of sand. I don't know what it was.'

There were days when Pranav could not look at his face in the mirror. He realised that he needed to talk to someone frankly about the colossal churn in his head. Someone he could trust. Pranav decided to speak with his boss. He had broken down in front of him a few times already, and found the experience strangely comforting. The older man not only listened to him patiently, he liked Pranav all the more for his willingness to re-examine everything, even when it damaged his memory of childhood and his sense of belonging. Sometimes there would be a late-night unburdening, when the words that came out made almost no sense—a series of long, convulsive phrases, compulsively spoken.

Around this time, an incident at work proved to be just the catharsis he was looking for. In the colony where Pranav's company was engaged in relief work, an ethnic clash erupted between two sects of Muslims, both followers of different schools of worship that originated in two different towns of Uttar Pradesh. One set were Barelvis, followers of the style of worship common in the town of Bareilly. The other were the Tablighi Jamaat, followers of the Deoband school, which was situated in that town. In the area where Pranav now worked, the two sects were engaged in a bitter turf war. One insisted that, since they had pumped in the greater share of money to build the resettlement colony, their style of worship must be followed at the local mosque. The other would not have it. Tempers were frayed on both sides. The situation reached bursting point and houses were set on fire.

It was just after the Friday prayers, and Pranav drove to the spot as soon as he heard what had happened. The police had already stepped in and made some arrests. But the tension needed to be diffused to prevent more violence from erupting. Pranav was calm and reasoned. He addressed both sides and said, 'Let's end this, or the police won't release your relatives on either side from jail.' The crisis blew over. He drove back to his office-cum-home and immediately sat down to write a report on the event. It was ostensibly about the ethnic clash between two groups of Muslims, but ended up helping him process his own prejudice.

'In my report, I wrote about the conflict over identity. They were also struggling with that. So it was a way for me to understand my own identity from a different space.' He added a line that ended up providing him with a massive release. It allowed him to forgive himself for a past he had very little control over. He wrote, 'Sometimes because of our identity we become perpetrators and sometimes we become victims. It's okay.' After writing that down, Pranav felt like it really was beginning to be okay. For the first time, he saw what he had been part of from a distance. And it made all the difference. He told himself that he would be alright.

And then there were days when he was not. Like the time he went home to his village. It was Diwali, a time when his family went to the Swaminarayan temple and propitiated the gods with a token representing their particular trade. Farmers offered sprigs of wheat. Some people offered home-made laddus. When Pranav's childhood friends arrived, he lacerated them with his newly acquired liberal outlook. 'If someone is an alcohol smuggler, can they deposit a bottle before the gods?' he asked. His friends looked incredulous as they said, 'This guy has gone completely mad.'

Years later, Pranav could see the effect his internal crisis was having on his work. 'It might have come out of frustration or fear. Or dominance,' he said later. 'Because I was in a very powerful position there. I was the boss. I could do whatever I liked. I might have exercised unnecessary power over someone.' The overzealousness with which he attacked religion was becoming a pattern, and was often in reaction to something that seemed perfectly innocuous to everyone else.

One of his teams had organised a film screening in a village, and a politician loosely affiliated with the Sangh was threatening to disrupt it. When Pranav found out about this, he flared up. 'What does the bastard think of himself, does his father own the village? We will all go there and make sure we screen it. The whole team!' he thundered. The team of fifteen people, half of them young girls, arrived at the village with Pranav. It was after dark. As soon as the film began to play, a group of drunk men turned up and started beating people up. Two girls from the team were hurt. Pranav had them escorted out quickly. Later, when he had time to reflect, Pranav realised that he had gone too far. Was it worth it, proving a point at the cost of his staff's safety?

For all this turmoil, at work, Pranav had begun to soar. His office was asked to manage a big-scale cricket tournament in a communally sensitive trading town. The real agenda was to build peace, and so the teams had to be half Muslim and half Hindu to qualify. The job wasn't just an organisational challenge; it required the mental agility of someone who could sell sand to an Arab. When youngsters heard about this proposal, their standard response was, 'This will never be possible.'

There were many hurdles to be crossed before the event could take off. For one thing, the ground selected for the final tournament had a mosque right in front and was close to a Muslim resettlement colony, so no Hindus wanted to take part. Pranav decided to camp in the area with his team at night, trying to find a way of getting through to people. The centre of town was a bus stand with a row of shops selling the ordinary and the essential—bicycle parts, medicines and soaps. Pranav stood at shop corners and open compounds, looking for kids who were as hooked to cricket as he had been growing up. To his surprise, he found that the town already had a mixed team that played in tournaments in other districts. All he needed to do was to entice its players to register for the tournament, and others would hopefully follow. But even with this groundwork in place, the going was tough. Not enough people were coming forward.

Pranav looked around for inspiration and saw a mason he knew well. He turned to him and asked, 'Tell me, how many villages do you work in?'

The unsuspecting man replied, 'I work in a lot of villages, around thirty possibly.'

This is what Pranav threw at him next: 'Can you form a cricket team with people from all those villages?'

The mason liked cricket and was thrilled to be asked. He came back a few weeks later with a mixed team that was ready to play.

As the tournament date drew closer and posters were put up everywhere, the town was suddenly alive and bursting with excitement. A formidable crowd gathered to watch. By the time the finals were played, Pranav noticed what the game had done to the town. 'We observed that slowly, slowly, the players' interaction with each other became more about the game and not who they are. Which is what we wanted,' he said, beaming. At the end of the tournament, a large silver cup was handed out to the winning team. But it was Pranav who had won something important and life-altering. The tournament had changed him, perhaps even more than the players. It told him what he needed to know most—that he could let go of his past and save himself.

Since the tournament had been such a smashing success, Pranav and his team were tasked with organising another one the following year, in 2004. 'The next year, without us saying anything, thirty-five teams came to us on their own,' Pranav stated proudly.

He allowed the cricket project to obliterate his personal space almost entirely. Only Vikram detected that there may have been more than one reason for Pranav to hide behind his work. That it could also have had something to do with a woman he was trying to forget. 'He had a girlfriend for a very long time. He liked her intensely and she was not responding,' Vikram revealed. Was this really true? Pranav never spoke about it. But perhaps the cricket had finally lifted his spirits enough so he could open himself up to feeling once again.

That was what it seemed like when Vikram got a call from Pranav right in the middle of the tournament, announcing that he was getting married. There had been no preamble, no build-up, no fanfare. It was a bolt from the blue, but Pranav made it sound as regular as the rolling out of the time-table for the next day's match. None of Pranav's other colleagues—people he spent days and nights with in the run-up to the tournament—knew. Vikram never asked him why he decided to marry, but thought aloud much later that perhaps the years away from home, the alienation, the loss of an entire world of the old and familiar had made Pranav lonely. It may have been what made him agree to this one imposition from the world he grew up in, of allowing his parents to find him a partner.

Pranav met thirty-five women at his parents' behest before finally meeting the one he wanted to marry. 'I didn't really want to get married,' he confessed. But one day, something within him changed, and he said to his parents, 'Okay, I will do it, what's the big deal?' The nonchalance was perhaps a cover for his fear at closing one door firmly and opening another. Having conceded some space to his parents, the rebel in Pranav resurfaced. He told his parents firmly, 'It will not be a religious ceremony. We will marry in court. There will be no big hungama. And I will come home for precisely one day. The day of the wedding. And go back to work the next day.' And that is precisely what he did. The morning after his wedding, he was back in office.

It was very close to the final day of the tournament. The pressure was high, and special security was needed for the celebrity chief guest. The district administration and police needed to be brought on board. And Pranav started the day by asking everyone to gather round for a quick meeting. With everyone present, he opened a box of mithai. 'Help yourselves to some sweets, everyone,' Pranav said. 'I got married yesterday.' His team was shocked. They put it down to his quirky personality—this was just the way he was.

By the time the third tournament was organised, the Sangh Parivar had noticed what was happening to the atmosphere in the area because of it. Some of their own children had played in mixed teams. This transformation threatened their politics. It was the year the tournament had reached its peak. A staggering sixty-four teams of young boys and another twenty all-girl teams signed up to compete. But when the final match was played, the Sangh found something innocuous to use against the game.

'A member from the winning team in his excitement probably picked up a flag from the dargah nearby and waved it in the air as a sign of victory,' Pranav explained. It was a green flag. A photo of this victory run was circulated. Pranav and his team were summoned to a local body meeting, where he was told, 'That was a Pakistani flag being waved. You are ruining the image of the whole district.' The local police had the perfect excuse to deny permission for any future tournaments. It could be a threat to law and order. Pranav was furious. This was not just a game, it was his whole life being stopped in its tracks. His professional battle with the state and its extended Hindu arm had now become intensely personal.

TWENTY-TWO

Suresh was going to jail. That was inevitable after he had bragged about 28 February on camera. It was his bragging, more than his brutality, that was instructive. Suresh had a captive audience that he was catering to with his violence and the retelling of it. They were his support base, his source of power, and the reason he told his stories with so much conviction. His primary audience was not the people who saw the surreptitiously taped sting broadcast on televisions across the country, but the mob and its silent supporters. The bragging was the whole point, making it amply clear to Suresh's supporters that his deeds were not an abomination. The problem was that he was careless enough to have been caught.

In 2007, when the Suresh tapes were broadcast, there was already a great big rotary in motion. The wheels had started to turn when the National Human Rights Commission tracked a couple of cases from 2002, including Naroda Patiya in which Suresh was implicated. The commission found major faults with the investigation† and took that to the Supreme Court. It passed an order asking for a fresh probe. When the case was opened up again, the press and public began to talk

---

† Manoj Mitta, *Modi & Godhra: The Fiction of Fact-Finding*, HarperCollins, 2014, p. 56.

about how the BJP government in Gujarat was protecting its leader Maya Kodnani. That her role had not been investigated by the state police. Because of the furore, these complaints were taken on board. The police was under tremendous pressure. And the Gujarat government, under Chief Minister Narendra Modi, was smarting from accusations that it had meddled with cases from 2002. Charges were framed against Kodnani; she resigned from her ministerial post and was arrested in April 2009. She was released on bail a month later, like the other accused. Almost a decade later, in April 2018, she was acquitted of all charges by the Gujarat High Court. But the fact that she was arrested at all sent shivers down Suresh's spine. If the state no longer protected its own minister, there was little chance that he would be spared a long jail term.

The trial began in 2009. The presiding judge, Jyotsna Yagnik, spent three years listening to depositions from both sides as a revised list of the accused was drawn up, a total of sixty-two persons, including Suresh. Each day that he was summoned to court, Suresh acted out the anger that the humiliation filled him with when he returned home. On one such occasion, he hurled the usual set of accusations at Farzana, of sleeping with other men behind his back. But this time, he accused her of sleeping with his own brother, and thrashed her with a lathi till it broke. At night, Farzana didn't say a word. But the next morning, after he left for court, she went straight to the panchayat in Chhota Chharanagar.

As a nomadic and criminalised community, the Chharas had always reposed more faith in their own council or panch than in the state. The council was meant to equally represent all sub-castes and groups amongst the Chharas. But like most institutions in the country, it had got corrupted over time. People had to deposit a sum of money to approach them for a hearing. Farzana managed to cobble up the requisite amount. She also phoned her mother and asked her to be present as a witness when the panch met.

Khatoonbibi arrived to support her daughter. And right in front of Suresh, Farzana and everyone gathered there, she spat at him, 'Did you accuse my daughter of sleeping with other men?' Then she added a punchline calculated to hit him where it hurt most: 'Why, are you unable to satisfy her?'

It appeared to Farzana that, for once, he was completely stumped. 'Well, the men in the area keep telling me she is out and about town with all sorts of people while I am away in court or in jail,' Suresh said.

Khatoonbibi was livid. 'You believe whatever rubbish people in the street say?'

The panch asked Farzana what she wanted, and she said in the clearest possible terms that she no longer wished to live with Suresh. 'It's finished,' Farzana said diffidently. '*Khallas ho gaya ab*. It's all over.'

Suresh did his usual act of getting down on his knees, apologising to Farzana, to Khatoonbibi and to the panch. He swore this would never happen again. Khatoonbibi looked at him and then thought about the kids. Both were still very young. She decided to persuade her daughter to relent and go back to him. She said to Farzana, 'Okay, drop it this last time. He's probably not going to stay free much longer.' Those words turned out to be prophetic, or at least an accurate assessment of where the case was headed. The tide had turned. The witnesses, 327 of them, many of whom were eyewitnesses, had waited eight long years and were finally being put on the stand to identify members of the mob.

Amongst them, waiting her turn eagerly, was Farida Bano Abdul Qadir Khalifa. She was a large and feisty woman, a few years older than Suresh, and had lived in Chharanagar since she was three months old. 'I spent my entire childhood there. I was married there. I had four children there—three boys and a girl,' Farida said. 'I was quite friendly with Suresh's sister, Sita.' The one who later ran away with a Muslim man, she clarified. She knew the family well, and lived right opposite their house. 'Suresh was a brat even as a kid. Always up to no good.' But so were other kids in Chhota Chharanagar. Farida's family had even given him a job at their mutton shop when he was about fourteen. 'He did a good job,' she said. 'He learned how to cut and clean the meat.' In fact, Farida said, they were on such good terms that, after a good round of thieving, Suresh often came by her house with a fat wad of notes and said to her, 'Keep this safe, Faridaben. I will pick it up tomorrow, after the booze has worn off.'

'He'd never count the money. It could be any amount, 5–10–15,000, anything. He'd just come pick it up when his head cleared the next morning,' Farida said. 'And I would tell him, don't you ever come to my house smelling like that again, and he would listen to me.'

Farida remembered an instance when Suresh and his three friends picked up a girl from the area in the middle of the night. 'He liked her and she didn't like him back, I think. We all slept on charpais outside our homes. So he arrived with his friends one night, covered her face and picked her up while she was sleeping.' The girl's parents were hysterical, but Suresh and his friends could not be found. Two days later, the girl came home sobbing and recounted how Suresh had raped her in the fields behind Chhota Chharanagar. Farida paused before adding a comment on what she felt this story said about Suresh. 'It was his fancy, that kind of wanton behaviour, you know. That's what Suresh did.'

A year before the violence, Farida Bano had moved out to the adjoining colony of Naroda Patiya to a gully called Husain Nagar Ki Chali. She then set up a tea stall at the intersection of the two colonies. The night of the Godhra train-burning, Husain Nagar was tense. The men running food carts nearby came up to Faridaben and said, 'It doesn't look good. We suggest you pack up and go home.' On the morning of 28 February, Farida saw a large knot of people hovering around the Noorani masjid across the road from her house. In it, amongst others she knew, was Suresh. He was unmistakable as he hobbled about with a sword in hand, dragging his bad leg with him. She also saw the gynaecologist–politician Maya Kodnani arrive on the scene. 'As soon as Mayaben left, the police started to fire into the crowd. Six people were injured by police bullets, and we went to pick them up and get them some medical attention,' she said.

Farida did the obvious thing by approaching a policeman for help. She wasn't prepared for his reply. 'Get out of here, today no Musalmaan will survive,' he told her. She ran back home, grabbed her kids and left for a safer zone. They kept moving towards the state reserve police quarters that abutted their colony. It was evening by then. On their way there, Farida saw a young boy jump off a balcony to escape the burning soda bottles that were being lobbed from the sky. He fell and fractured his legs. As he lay still in the middle of the road, Farida saw Suresh and his gang close in. They put the boy into an autorickshaw, poured kerosene all over and lit a match. It went up in flames, the boy screaming inside until he died. This was the story Farida had been waiting so long to tell.

As the appointed day of the hearing arrived, she began to be courted by various people whom she had named in her police complaint. A couple of them called her to their office by the Kubernagar railway line, just where Chharanagar and Naroda Patiya meet. 'They sat me down and served me a cold drink,' Farida said, smiling at the memory. 'I drank it. And then asked them—tell me, how can I help you?' The accused persons sat her down and explained nervously that, since their names were in the police files, would she be able to do them a favour and not identify them in court? Farida had spent eight long years working towards this day. She had lived in a relief camp. She had lost family members. She had been to the police for the first time in her life. She had a plan.

She looked at them and smiled coolly. 'I don't know what you're talking about,' she said.

'But, Ben, your name is listed here as a witness,' they replied.

'Read what it says,' she went on.

They read the name listed in the file—Farida Bano Abdul Qadir Khalifa—and then relaxed, just as Farida had intended. This wasn't the Farida they were sitting in front of, they thought. Her name was Farida Bano Shabbir Hussain Sheikh. What they did not know was that Farida had divorced her husband and married again. Therefore, she now had a new name with the suffix of her second husband. But they thought, she was an old neighbour. Surely she would not have reported them to the police? Could the police have got the name wrong? Perhaps there was one less witness to worry about. Farida encouraged these thoughts and added suggestively, 'There are so many Faridas. I am certainly not the only one around. This person could be anybody.'

When the trial began, Farida met Suresh and the others

in the court premises. They greeted each other cordially. Suresh asked her if she would like some chai, and so she had some. She was offered some tobacco powder next, and she had some of that as well. As the moment of truth arrived, Farida sensed a distinct uneasiness amongst her lawyers. 'She's having chai with those people and chatting with them. She's up to something. She may turn hostile in court,' they probably said behind her back.

When her name was called, Farida walked into court confidently. She wore an outward mask of coolness while inwardly exploding with excitement. 'How would you like to identify the accused—by name or in person?' she was asked.

'I will go up to each one, point them out, make them stand and identify them by name,' was Farida's reply.

'You should have seen the look on their faces,' she said, her eyes burning bright.

Suresh was the second of the twenty-five people she identified in court that day. He was incensed. They had drunk tea together. It made his blood boil to see how he had been played. Muslims could not be trusted. They were all the same, he thought. On days like this, when he got back home, all he could see when he looked at Farzana was that she was Muslim, just like the rest. 'It's all because of you that I am in jail,' he said.

'As if offering tea was supposed to make them change their minds,' Farzana said later, rolling her eyes.

On 31 August 2012, Suresh was handed a thirty-one-year jail sentence for murder and rape. Khatoonbibi's prophecy had come true.

TWENTY-THREE

After the shutting down of the cricket tournament, Pranav
was faced once again with the old existential questions.
Now, with the single most revitalising force in his life—the
cricket tournament—yanked from underfoot by a reactionary
administration, Pranav was lost. What was the point of all
the work he had done to change things if it was going to be
systematically undone?

In December 2007 another shadow loomed large—the
elections in Gujarat. Pranav was following the political
campaigns of both major parties closely. He was hoping
that the work done amongst communities in the villages
would result in waning support for the party in power, the
BJP. He basked in the surround sound of civil society groups
that continually said to each other that the BJP's days were
numbered. People had seen through the hollow promises
of the present government and its extended network of
hardline Hindu propagandists. But Pranav also had a nagging
suspicion that they might be wrong. That the Hindutva
propaganda persisted because it worked, and that it may just
be what people would vote for. It was a terrifying thought.

In this phase, Pranav's visits to his village were becoming
more and more painful. He no longer belonged—it was
impossible to acknowledge that feeling, even to himself,
and equally impossible not to. It all came tumbling out in
conversations with his father.

'Why don't you sell this house, this land, and move to the university town with me where I have bought a flat?' Pranav said.

His father was taken aback. 'Are you mad? I am never going to sell this land—the blood and sweat of my ancestors. You go if you want to. Do what you like,' he said, visibly upset.

Another time, Pranav declared to his father, 'There are two kinds of people who pray to god. Those who don't believe in themselves enough. And those who have sinned. And I am neither. So I don't need prayers for now.'

His father was forced to ask again—was his son crazy? 'This is not the way to speak.'

But Pranav was on a roll. 'You know this bullshit you guys keep saying about what you will get in your next birth for being good and all? Where is the proof? Tell me.' It was as if he was at one of his workshops, reorienting his family in the desperate hope that they would travel with him to the place he was at. A rationalist and an atheist. He didn't want to be there alone.

But alone he was, even in his workplace. The Muslims he sat with after hours were every bit as devout as his own family. Out of solidarity, Pranav sometimes fasted with them in the days leading up to Eid and broke bread when they did. But over those meals, he was unable to contain himself. He provoked a colleague he was close to, 'Why don't you drop the five times a day prayer?' To others he would raise questions of gender inequality in Islam. 'Why do women have to wear the hijab?'

'The relationship was very close, so they couldn't say fuck off. They had to engage,' Pranav said, cackling. But it wasn't funny. His new world contained some of the same prejudices as his old, and they blew up in his face when he least expected it. The conflict between the Barelvis and Tablighi Jamaat was on the boil again. This time it engulfed Pranav. Municipal elections were held in the area and a candidate that Pranav was friendly with won. His opponents began to spread lies about Pranav. That he had conspired to make the other side lose. 'The losing candidate even held a protest rally against me with fifty or sixty of his supporters,' he said.

In the resettlement colony he was working in, the two sects expected Pranav to mediate their conflict, but he refused. That did not go down well.

The constant conflict was beginning to wear him down. 'I got fed up. I said to myself—with whom am I working and for what?' At these times, the midnight calls to his boss kept him together. But it was not enough.

Pranav decided to live further away to put some physical distance between the people he was working with and himself, hoping that it would take away some of the stress. He moved to a city some distance from work, and drove sixty-five kilometres to work on his trusty bike each day, reaching home by 8.30 on most nights. One such evening, he was parking his bike when it occurred to him that he had absolutely no recollection of the ride. 'There was stress. A lot of churning. But I was probably thinking something that I could not recall,' he said later. Alarmingly, even after he sat down for six hours, and tried to picture his bike ride, there was only blankness. 'I remembered chewing on some tobacco and crossing a factory very close to work. Until then I was conscious. Then, nothing,' he said, the panic rising in his face as he described that time. It was becoming impossible, dangerous even, to continue like this.

While he was making up his mind about what to do,

the Gujarat state elections were held. Pranav was tense. He did not want the Sangh Parivar to gain more ground than it already had. If the BJP won, it would be a vote for Hindutva. For saffronisation. The build-up to the election was so intense in Pranav's head, it was as if his entire life depended on it. He needed to head out of town with a few friends to drink in order to cope. His friend Vikram accompanied him on this trip. 'We were not watching the results on TV as far as I can remember,' he said. 'It was some loudspeaker announcing the results.' Of a total of 182 seats in the state assembly, the BJP won 70 per cent. Vikram described Pranav's slow shutdown after. 'In two hours, the whole thing was down the drain. There was no reaction. There was frustration. Like shit, whatever. *Paagal, kaise isko?* This is madness, how could they? But nothing more than that.'

Pranav wanted to leave, to get as far away as possible from the work. It was all too painful. But he was responsible for many people.

There was one person in particular that he could not let down. The woman whose case his office had been handling since 2002, whose story of being attacked by the mob and left for dead was the biggest motivator in his work. Pranav's primary task was to manage a long list of witnesses. To keep track of their whereabouts and make sure they were told when they needed to appear in court to testify. It sounded easy; it was anything but. The case—transferred out of Gujarat to avoid governmental manipulation—was being heard at a special court in Mumbai. When witnesses had to testify, they needed to be informed well in time and taken to Mumbai to be put on the stand.

It was an atmosphere pregnant with the possibility of money. 'They had already lost everything. So they wanted to get whatever they could from wherever. And we were not in a position to give them any money,' Pranav explained. On the other hand, he said, 'They thought ki yeh hamara case hai, this is our case. You have to give us something.' Pranav's office tried everything from the conventional to the seemingly ridiculous to ensure that the witnesses stayed with the case. 'We had one guy stationed in the colony where most of them lived, to keep track of them full time. His work was to do no work at all,' Pranav said, laughing. He had to make sure he knew where the witnesses were at all times. But he couldn't be seen hanging around suspiciously, doing nothing. So he was asked to start a library and run various vocational training classes.

Despite that, there were a few occasions when everyone in Pranav's office felt like they were having a collective heart attack. Two days before a witness was due to take the train to Mumbai, he went missing. After a thorough search, Pranav's colleague, who lived in the resettlement colony, found him hiding in a relative's house. When they tracked him down, he asked for money. Pranav instructed his colleague to bring him to the company office. 'I'll handle it from there,' he said. When the witness arrived, Pranav told him there was no money on offer, but he was welcome to call the company director and ask him directly. That diffused the situation for the moment. But there were others.

For advice, Pranav turned to an influential leader who had built the colony where the witnesses lived. 'Don't worry,' the man said as he got into his car and asked Pranav to jump in too. They drove down to the colony in question. People recognised the car and gathered around.

Before Pranav and his colleagues knew what was happening, a member from the leader's entourage whipped out some hockey sticks from the boot of the car and started to beat up the crowd that had gathered there. As they ran for cover, the leader hollered after them, 'You bastards! These people have put their lives on hold for you guys. For justice to be done in your case. And you turn around and demand money? How dare you?' he thundered. 'If any of you asks for a bribe again, I will come back here with a bulldozer and raze to the ground all the houses I have built for all of you. Is that clear?'

Pranav waited for the crowd to clear and turned to the leader, shaken. 'This isn't how you deal with people. What have you done?' But the leader wasn't interested in a sermon on what was politically correct. He turned to Pranav and replied, 'If you have any further trouble getting these people to court, all you have to do is pick up the phone and call me.'

Despite the devastating election result and conflict within the Muslim colonies, there was such an avalanche of work and so many lives at stake that Pranav found no time to stop and think. Until it all finally came crashing down over the central issue in his new world—religion and identity. Pranav's office had organised a large training programme in the city of Vadodara, and he was required to bring his staff and extended network of volunteers with him. He told everyone how crucial it was for them to be there, and that they all needed to assemble at the railway station on the appointed day at 8.30 p.m. When that night arrived, it was nearly 8.30 and nobody had turned up, except for one shame-faced colleague, Nasirbhai.*

By 8.45 p.m., Pranav was getting frantic. He was trying to call everyone who was meant to be on the train, but their cell-phones were switched off. 'What's going on, yaar? The train is about to leave,' Pranav said.

'Nobody will be coming,' Nasirbhai said gently.

Pranav's eyes were wide with astonishment. 'What? Why?'

Nasir spelt it out. 'Well, there's been some talk in the community for a while now about you. And everyone has been instructed to stay away. Even if it means losing their jobs.'

The accusation that Pranav was on the side of one sect of Muslims and not the other was rearing its ugly head again. Word had gone around that he had not given people time off during Ramzan, and had deliberately held workshops, meetings and even out-of-town projects at precisely that time. That he was unmindful of what it was like for a Muslim to have to work a full day while fasting.

That there was conflict was bad enough. The nature of the accusations broke Pranav's heart. By this time, work on the big riot case was over. His responsibilities on other contracts, including the cricket event, were done. He was now married, and had a son. It was time to quit this job and move on. The job had meant everything to him. It had taught him how to think and how to live. It had replenished his soul. But he couldn't take it any longer. And he could not face his boss either, nor allow him to hear his voice over the phone, broken and weak. Pranav texted him instead: 'I have resigned. Tomorrow morning please send someone to take charge.' Then he switched the phone off.

His boss immediately asked a senior colleague whom Pranav liked and respected to go down to the local office and meet him. She flew down from Bangalore. 'It was emotional,' Pranav said, underplaying the moment. 'We had a huge discussion.' But he knew that something had snapped. There was no way back in. He moved back to the university town where he had bought a flat. And for six or seven months, he did absolutely nothing. He didn't even tell his wife he had quit.

TWENTY-FOUR

After winning the local election by a massive margin, Dungar was made block president, or taluka pramukh. For once, he saw what it was like to be looked up to. Everyone needed him across the sixteen villages that made up the five blocks he was in charge of. They went to him for tubewell funds, or to build a road, or just for the use of the raw power he had in his grasp to sort out a dispute or settle scores with an enemy. He was already the king of schemes. He decided it was about time he explored its full potential. The villages he represented politically were parched lands. So, Dungar put in a request for money to drill borewells and handpumps. Two borewells and handpumps for every locality in the block. 'I knew the block development officer,' Dungar explained with some pride. 'I got him to clear these projects.'

If applying for funds through various means resulted in some good work getting off the ground, it was a bonus, but not critical. The money being collected was an end in itself. For instance, Dungar had a factory set up to make urinals and toilets because the government of Gujarat was promoting it. Toilets for all. 'I had 35,000 pots installed,' Dungar said with some satisfaction. It was an incredible number for a block that consisted of 28,000 households at the time. The catch was that they were hardly ever used. In fact, they were broken from disuse within a few years. 'Because there was no water to run them,' Dungar said, suddenly sombre. This was an area with an acute water shortage. With no taps to fill water to wash after use and, more importantly, no water to run the flush, the toilets were nothing more than enclosed boxes with piles of dry faeces. Toxic containers that were eminently unusable and the very opposite of the stated purpose of the project. They were unhygienic.

A former colleague had observed how Dungar worked the system. This man had lived in Dungar's home and was a colleague in the NGO that had set up rehabilitation projects in the area. He said, 'If Dungar applied for a project worth 1,000 rupees, some 500 would be what he actually spent on it.' The rest were bloated bills raised to feed his ever-growing appetite for power and money. It was the surest way out of the insecurity and low self-esteem that, despite everything, still persisted. Dungar was aware of how fragile his new edifice was. One false move and there were many waiting in the wings to pull him down. Money was a buffer, perhaps the only buffer. If there was another way to do politics, it was not one he had access to. Even his neighbour and critic, with whom Dungar had a falling out, acknowledged that this was how things were done.

Dungar's long-time friend Roop Sinh explained how hard it was to break out of the drudgery of working the cornfields every day. The seeds needed to be placed at the right distance from each other, the bed in which they were placed properly levelled. The soil under each sapling had to be turned and loosened from time to time to prevent water from collecting in one place and ruining the crop. This meant having to work bent over all day in the hottest months of the year till the skin off his back was scalded in the heat. Roop Sinh had tried to find a way out of farming and failed. He had paid a big fat bribe of Rs 25,000 at one time to an agent who had promised to get him a job with the police. 'The guy kept me hanging for a year and then delivered nothing. So my money was sunk and I was still jobless.' When an opportunity to get past that presented itself, only the very stupid would walk away from it. He admired Dungar for making the most of what came his way.

'I did work worth forty-five crore rupees in that phase,' Dungar said triumphantly.

It was as if he had scrambled up a tall, shaky mahuda tree and was now losing perspective. What if another tree grew taller, blocking his view, putting him in the shade? He looked around, and there was a bigger, taller figure in his path. The member of the state legislature from the area, a well-established BJP leader. He had once been a mentor and someone who had helped Dungar get noticed by the party. Now he was standing in the way. As his five-year term as block president came to an end in 2010, Dungar could not help thinking about this fact. His leader and former mentor was now a competitor, and if Dungar wanted to rise further, he needed to eliminate the man politically.

'I had a massive showdown with this guy around the time my term ended,' Dungar said. 'I told him straight that I was doing whatever he told me to, but that it wasn't helping me in the end at all.'

Another avenue seemed to be opening up, and Dungar calculated how he could use it to bring his rival down.

In the political chessboard that was Gujarat, the man at the helm of affairs, Narendra Modi, had done exactly what Dungar was planning to. He had eliminated a big tree that was standing in his way—his rival and the former chief minister of the state, Keshubhai Patel. Modi had stepped over him to win two successive elections. After ten years at the top, he towered over every other leader in Gujarat. A decade later, that big tree had grown new roots. By the winter of 2012, Keshubhai had a new party to his name. He was looking for local leaders to partner with, and Dungar decided to jump ship.

The first part of his elaborate plan was to win Keshubhai's trust. An opportunity presented itself when the new party wanted to organise a large rally where Dungar lived. It was an uphill task because the local administration joined hands with the BJP to make it impossible for Keshubhai to function. Farmers across the region were instructed not to host the event on their land. Dungar swung into action, doing what he was best at—brokering deals. He offered a farmer he knew Rs 5,000 to sign an agreement that he would hold the rally. However, when the papers went to the office of the district revenue officer, he demanded to meet the farmer in question on the pretext that his signature could be forged. The farmer got scared and did not turn up. The date of the event was drawing close, and pressure was mounting. Dungar called an influential leader in Keshubhai's party and told him what had happened. The leader, a master of manoeuvres, told Dungar not to worry. 'I will send in the press.' A deluge of journalists from various television channels swamped the revenue office, demanding to know why a rally of tribal persons was being blocked. Meanwhile, Dungar was busy brokering a deal with another farmer. This time he increased the reward five-fold to Rs 25,000. The deal was done. The papers were signed, and the district administration had no choice but to allow the rally to take place.

But all of this was only Dungar's way of setting the stage for the real battle. 'Keshubhai heaped praise on me once the rally was held. Because so many people turned up. So, I became close to him. I could call him directly, whenever I liked,' Dungar said. Having won the leader's admiration and trust, Dungar now canvassed for his former mentor being offered a plum position in the new party. The rival was duly approached to jump ship and he did. This automatically eliminated him from the BJP. But given the flip-flop of political loyalties, Dungar wanted to ensure that his political nemesis would never be considered by the BJP again.

He surreptitiously taped conversations in which the man had bragged about how he had 'Modi in his pocket' and had the recording sent to Modi's office. The rival was trapped. He would never get a BJP ticket again, and Dungar knew he wouldn't stand much of a chance in the other party either. Keshubhai was a spent force; in the 2012 election, his party won just two seats. Dungar's gamble had paid off. His opponent was now in the political wilderness. For the moment, so was Dungar, because he had jumped ship to oust his rival.

But he had factored this into his plan, and had left a back channel open with the BJP throughout the period he was courting Keshubhai. Party insiders had a grudging admiration for Dungar's skulduggery and political dexterity. These were the real leadership qualities that every single party was looking for. Or at least, that was what Dungar had hedged his bets on. With the reputation of his rival suitably sullied, the road ahead looked like it was clear.

But not everything panned out the way he planned. While Dungar's mind was occupied with complex political jugglery, his wife had taken him to court. They had been living apart for the most part since they were married and now she demanded maintenance. 'The case lasted three years,' Dungar said, frowning. 'Then our entire community got together and talked her out of it. She came around eventually, and lives in my parents' house now,' Dungar said. Then, realising that this was not painting an appropriate picture of him, he quickly added, 'And I get her whatever she wants.'

In the open courtyard outside his father's house at the bottom of the hill, on most afternoons, Dungariben* could be seen sorting out the tuar dal or corn. Separating the good seeds from the rotten ones, one at a time. Her head covered with a ghunghat, eyes and face barely visible. Her sunken face and wrinkled arms and wafer-thin frame hid years of anger and steely determination. When she had taken her husband to court, she had wanted the world to see the raging fire within. But now Dungariben had capitulated. Their eldest child, a girl with a long plait and bright eyes, was studying to take her class twelve exams again. Their son, a young man in trendy clothes, drove an ambulance service in the area for a living. The ambulance was one of Dungar's fleet of five cars, which he had started to rent out to the state. Politics was indeed good business.

TWENTY-FIVE

Suresh was back in jail, smarting from the fact that the Muslims he despised so much had finally succeeded in having him put away for thirty-one years. It was clear that this time there would be no bail. His wife became the object of his rage, which was now worse than it had ever been. It was all Farzana's fault, Suresh said each time she came to visit him.

'It's because of you that I am motherfucked like this,' Suresh spat at her.

Farzana turned around and spat right back. 'You got what you deserve.'

Sure enough, she paid for having answered back. Suresh got time out of jail by applying for a few weeks of parole. Farzana welcomed him home, and warmed up some water for his bath. Suresh sat and chatted with his aunt and uncle. At night, after everyone had left, he turned to Farzana, drunk. 'So I got what I deserved, huh?' he said. Shwaaaaap, the rubber whip in his hand came down on her waist, then her back. 'It took out some of my flesh each time,' Farzana remembered. 'I fell off the bed while he was whipping me, but he wouldn't stop.' Their daughter Richie ran across to Suresh's chachi, pounding on their door, crying. Radhaben got up, went over to the house and finally got Suresh to stop. She took Farzana back to her home for the night.

By 2 a.m., Suresh's anger had worn off, and he stumbled

across to Radhaben's. 'Where is that Musalmaani? Send her home, the kids are crying,' he said to his aunt. Farzana did as she was told. She went back home and put the kids to bed. 'Where are you hurt, let me put some ice. Let me put some antiseptic cream,' Suresh said to her once the children were asleep. Farzana refused outright. She asked a relative and neighbour in the area to put some ice on her wounds instead. 'When she saw how badly I was bruised, she started crying,' Farzana said.

Once Suresh was back in jail, the wild oscillations in his moods continued. There were days when he sent home drawings and cards full of love notes and messages. He even planned their daughter Richie's wedding engagement. Farzana had bought herself a beautiful pink lehenga for the occasion. And a bright blue one for her daughter. It was a time to dream—that her daughter would have the romance she had once hoped for. Tears rolled down her face when she saw how stunning Richie looked. Suresh had got leave from jail for the occasion. And he was there, crying alongside, a mess of emotions as he looked at his grown-up daughter. The engagement broke soon after. 'The boy turned out to be alcoholic and violent. If Richie had married him, her life would have been as good as over,' Farzana explained.

In June 2015, when Suresh was out on a fifteen-day parole, he had no idea that this would be the very last time he would be with his wife. Farzana was in pain. She had a knot in her chest, so as soon as Suresh was home, he took her to the doctor. And then it occurred to him that he could use his wife's illness to have his leave extended. Once they reached the hospital, he instructed Farzana to have herself admitted as a patient so he could use her illness to apply for an extension of his time out from jail. She had no choice but to comply. He ran to the court, armed with the hospital papers and had his time out of jail extended by a week. In the hospital, Farzana's nerves were frayed. The nurses kept coming to take fresh blood samples every now and then, making her very nervous. 'Will you get me out of here, or should I just run away to my ammi's house?' she said to him. Suresh finally relented and brought her home. And then he slipped into the familiar pattern of hurling accusations at her. 'Just give me a divorce. Why do you keep me if I am sleeping around as you say?' Farzana retorted angrily.

At night, Farzana refused to sleep with Suresh. 'I have my period. Not now,' she said to him. He stepped out of the house and returned a few hours later, stinking of alcohol. 'You don't have your period in your ass, right,' he said in a menacing tone. And then he pinned her down and tied her legs to the bed-post. He tied her hands behind her back, then tied her mouth with her dupatta and shoved himself into her bottom. She screamed. Their daughter who was sleeping in the aunt's dhaba next door woke up with a start.

'What's happened, Papa?' she cried out.

'It's nothing, your mother is just screaming for the heck of it. That's all.' He covered Farzana's mouth again and threatened her, 'If you make a sound I will pulverise you.'

As he raped Farzana, he smoked a cigarette and stubbed out the butt on the back of her hand. Right on top of the dark green Om-shaped tattoo they had once got together.

After he was done, Suresh went to sleep. And Farzana went to the toilet. 'It hurt when I tried to pee,' she said. 'And there was blood as well.' She cried until 5 a.m. and then packed her clothes into a bundle and left for her mother's, her mind made up never to return.

TWENTY-SIX

6 a.m. People in Jamalpur's Ram Rahim Ka Tekra were just about rubbing the sleep from their eyes, rolling up their mattresses and getting ready to start the day when Farzana got home. Her mother and brother were surprised to see her that early in the morning. It was apparent that something had happened, and Farzana wouldn't say what. Talking to her brother about rape was out of the question, but she found it too humiliating to tell even her mother. Farzana waited for a day, and then when her mother started to suggest that she return to Chharanagar, she had an outburst. 'If you tell me to go back there I will kill myself,' she yelled between sobs.

When Khatoonbibi was apprised of the truth, she was black with rage. There was no question of sending her daughter back. But not all of Farzana's family was on her side, especially the sister Suresh had once courted. Opinions kept swinging back and forth between, 'Well, she stepped into the fire, now let her deal with it, she can't come running back when she feels like it' to 'No, she cannot go back there, she must stay here in Jamalpur'. It was a classic case of the family being resentful because a woman member had been too wilful. When one of the sisters threatened to boycott her parents' home if Farzana was allowed to stay, Khatoonbibi finally laid down the law. 'Look,' she said, 'I am keeping her here. Whoever wants to come and visit me is welcome. And whoever wants to stay away, go right ahead.' Then she took the irate sister aside and reasoned with her separately. 'So what if Farzana strayed by marrying Suresh? She is returning to the fold now. To the faith.'

It was settled. Farzana would stay. It was going to be a struggle. Her parents lived in a one-room tenement the size of a middle-class kitchen. It barely accommodated a single bed, a tiny sink and tap, and a few pots and pans. And it housed Farzana's parents, her younger brother, and his wife and child. Now they would also have to make room for her. The women slept indoors—one on the bed, the others on the floor next to the sink. The men slept outside. But Khatoonbibi finally had her daughter back, and she was not going to let her go. Not even when Suresh and his cousin turned up a day later.

This time Suresh's pleas and the steady stream of apologies did not work. He even tried telling Khatoonbibi that she could wait until his parole was over and he was back in jail, and then send Farzana home.

'My family will split up, Ammi. What about the kids?' Suresh said, hands folded, begging.

'Well, you should have thought about that before you did what you did,' was the firm reply.

The next day, Suresh's aunt turned up. Khatoonbibi and Farzana remained unmoved. The following week, when the aunt returned, Farzana exploded. 'This is what he did to me,' she hollered at Radhaben, and told her about the rape. By now, a crowd of curious neighbours and strangers had gathered around to participate in the public showdown.

Which made it worse when the aunt said, 'Oh well, all men do that. When our men do what they like with us, we don't go around broadcasting it to the whole world.'

Farzana was too stunned to speak.

But Khatoonbibi stepped in now. 'Your men may be doing this kind of thing, ours don't. And we don't stand for this kind of shit either, unlike you lot.'

In the next few days, Farzana had some crucial decisions to make. First, the kids. She told both of them over the phone that she was not returning to Chharanagar, and they were welcome to come and live with her. 'I said I will rent another place near my parents' and work in homes or get some sort of job, and that they could stay with me, but they firmly refused,' she said. Richie was seventeen and Vivian was fifteen. Both earned a tidy sum of about Rs 30,000 a month through various trades, including—their mother suspected—selling liquor. 'They sold English,' said Farzana; not the local hooch made in plastic barrels, but the pricier and better Indian-made foreign liquor. Giving that up for a life of squalor in the vicinity of their grandparents was unacceptable to them. Besides, Farzana gathered, they felt betrayed by their mother. 'We will never leave our father and come to you. You've ditched him, but we won't,' they said to her. Farzana said they probably believed Suresh: 'They thought he hasn't done anything, and that I just took advantage of the fact that he was in jail.'

The other big decision Farzana made was to take Suresh to court. To file a complaint against him with the police for rape and domestic violence, and also file for divorce. This was a process that took several months and meant overcoming a considerable amount of trepidation. In the beginning, there was only a bottomless pit of anger that Farzana didn't know how to process. All she knew for certain was that she did not want to go back, and that she wanted to end her marriage. So she reached out to people she had been meeting—friends and acquaintances who she thought knew more of the world that she did. The advice she got was unequivocal. That she should file a complaint with the police while the wounds from the cigarette butts were still fresh and there was visible evidence of her having been attacked.

So far, to Farzana, the police had only stood for fear. They were the people who turned up at odd hours to beat up and arrest Suresh. But the thought that he might come after her and kill her when he was out on parole next scared her more than anything else. It finally made her turn to the police for help. Her friends and family explained that it might prevent Suresh from getting parole again. It would keep her safe. It would also allow her to make a strong case against him that she could use to secure a divorce. Eventually, she was ready to take Suresh to court. But she needed a lawyer for that. Someone who would take her case for free.

After hunting high and low, asking Muslim clerics, NGOs and welfare organisations, she found the right person: a lawyer called Shabana Mansuri, who was stern, poised and purposeful. She had considerable experience working with 2002 victims and also various cases of domestic violence. As she talked to Farzana across a broken table at the Bhadra court in the old part of Ahmedabad city, she wanted to know if her client had made up her mind. 'Are you sure you won't have a change of heart when you see Suresh in court, or your kids, and decide to drop the case?' she asked Farzana repeatedly.

The clat-clat of old typewriters punctuated the air. Lawyers and their assistants in black coats, and clients of various descriptions sat on metal chairs chained to desks. This was the way things were in the sessions court. No one could be trusted with even a beat-up chair. The desks bore the cracks of time and decrepitude, and exposure to too much sun. Much of the business was conducted in an open courtyard, exposed to the elements and the occasional bird dropping. A cat sprung up on the tree overhead.

Farzana looked her lawyer straight in the eye and said firmly, 'No, I am very sure I don't want to go back.'

The frown on Shabana's face dissolved into a broad smile. 'Okay. I'll draw up the papers.'

TWENTY-SEVEN

It's funny how the darkest moments of Pranav's life were also the most illuminating. Once he quit his job, the churn subsided and there was a quiet calm. And tucked away in that calm was the realisation that he was free to let it all go. To let go of the hurt religion had caused him by putting him in the wrong place in 2002. To forgive himself, to allow himself his imperfect past so that he could allow other people theirs.

It came to him from the everyday, from time spent at home observing his wife. She prayed, and watching her at it wasn't a hurtful, disconcerting feeling. It didn't make him bristle with anger. He found that sometimes he needed to just let things be, to let something outside his belief system affect him without joining the dots back to a world of pain. 'You cannot disconnect yourself from the entire world, and why should you,' he asked. 'Then what will you have left to talk about?' His eyes were bright as he explained the process. 'Earlier, I used to think, what should I say, what can we talk about? She does not have the exposure I have. But now we are at a stage where we accept each other for what we are,' he said.

With his son, however, he was less accommodating. When he was seven years old, the boy had asked Pranav, 'Papa, is there a god?' The reply was a firm, 'No.'

On festival days, when he saw his son at his mother's

puja table, Pranav chided him gently. 'If there is no god, who are you praying to?'

His son replied, 'Mama said to do this.'

Pranav thought for a second and tried to say something that would meet his wife's beliefs halfway, so their child would be a little less confused. 'Rama, Krishna, Christ—they were all good people.'

His son didn't give up. 'So I can be like them?'

The father was amused. 'Yes, you can. You just have to do some good work and tell it to as many people as possible,' he said sarcastically.

Even as he said that, Pranav realised he had to stop projecting his own fears onto his son. 'What if he turns out to be a typical Gujarati?' he would worry. 'I have the least influence on him because of the little time I get with him. He has these huge inputs from my wife, my parents and brother. They haven't changed.' Then he would stop and remind himself, 'If I could change, so can he.'

But the obsessive-compulsive desire to fix his son's worldview was hard to put away. When the boy came home from school, Pranav would check his diary for notes from the teacher on homework and tasks for the next day. Just before Ganesh Chaturthi, it had the following instructions: 'Please bring two laddus for the class celebration.' He said to his son, 'Tomorrow, why don't you also ask your teacher whether you need to bring anything for the class celebration of Eid that is coming up next? And also tell her that she should inform you in advance if you need to bring some mutton for the celebration, because I will have to go to the meat shop in the walled city to get it.' The son dutifully asked his teacher exactly that. The teacher replied as Pranav expected—'No, there won't be any need for meat. We are not doing anything for Eid in class.' The son returned, went straight to his father and asked why Eid was not being celebrated. Pranav was thrilled to have put the question in his child's head.

Now that he had quit his job, Pranav had time to stop and think. He had changed so much from the time he first started working. From the hard-shelled rebel hitting out at the world, he had turned into someone who allowed himself to be visibly affected by people. 'I started recognising that I can cry,' Pranav said. 'In front of one or two friends,' he added. 'And I didn't feel angry ki, what kind of man is this, is he crazy or what? How can he be a man and cry like this? I didn't feel like that anymore.'

Still, he found it tough to acknowledge to his wife that he had no job. 'I used to work from home as a consultant. And my wife saw that it wasn't necessary for me to go to an office every day at nine o'clock, so she must have guessed that I had quit,' he said, slightly embarrassed. After about seven months, Pranav realised that he missed his work. He could not go back to the town where he had organised the cricket tournaments and built resettlement colonies for Muslims. But he still wanted to work with young people on issues of human rights and identity. He went back to his former boss for advice.

His old mentor was thrilled to see Pranav again. He listened patiently, stroked his chin, peered over his glasses and suggested the younger man make two important shifts. The first was geographical, to a different city, with different sights and sounds and associations. The second was hierarchical. He suggested to Pranav that, instead of being a soldier on the ground, he could lead from the top, in a company that did the kind of work he was interested in.

So Pranav moved cities and jobs. A tempering process

was clearly underway; it had even started to change the way he looked. Once, his deep-set eyes had blazed with fire and anguish. Now some of that fire was gone. The excitement was contained, held back by a circumspection acquired over time, and it sometimes came across as a cool, glassy look. Except to his mentor, who knew what those eyes concealed.

His metamorphosis, and the experience of breaking down and rebuilding himself in the eight years between 2002, when he first started working, and 2010, allowed Pranav to see uniquely—both this side and that. No one and nothing could take that away from him. And since this was an unusual and rare space to be in, Pranav decided to craft his new work around it.

He created a new training programme. It didn't have a name, but it may as well have been called 'In which you shed your old skin'. Pranav would start by asking young recruits what about themselves they felt proudest of. The youngsters, eager to please, would raise their hands and call out answers. Pranav put them down on the whiteboard in two separate columns. One list was always very long and contained words like family, background, school, community, place and country. The other list had words like scholarship, cricket cup, first prize. Pranav would then turn to the class. 'Do you see something? Why have I put down what you've said in these two lists like this?' he would ask before he threw the punchline.

'We are often proud of things that we have had absolutely no control over. That we have not decided. For instance, I did not decide to be born in a Hindu household.' The audience would go silent. Pranav went on, 'And this is the beginning of most of our problems in this world. They are based on choice-less identities. Hardly any of our conflicts are centred on choice-based identities.'

He explained the difference. Those whose sense of self rests on caste, religion, class or gender are stuck with an identity that they were born with. Over which they have had no control. Those who said they were proud of winning a cricket match or coming first in class or being a doctor had moved away from what they were born with, and into identities based on what they had done for themselves. 'You grow when you can base your identity on things from the second list instead of the first,' Pranav ended, pointing to the lists once again.

It was a formidable exercise. Those watching said it was as if a tornado had swept through the class. Pranav was talking to people who came from the same background as him, with similar unresolved questions they didn't even know were sitting inside them. He knew how to pull them out. He had lived on both sides now.

At a training session in the dreamy, touristy Mount Abu in Rajasthan, a group of three young boys approached Pranav for some advice. 'We've formed a youth group,' they said. 'And we were about to register it when a larger organisation found out about us and suggested that we run their operation instead. What do you think?'

Pranav asked them what the organisation was called, knowing what they would say.

'It's the Rashtriya Swayamsevak Sangh, the RSS,' they replied.

Exactly as Pranav had anticipated.

'Well, why don't you do one thing,' Pranav told them. 'Tell me what are your dreams for the group you've created. What do you want to do?'

The boys replied, 'We want to work amongst people and for people. We want to do something with our lives.'

'Okay, then why don't you go and find out a bit more about the RSS? Read up about them on the internet. Look at their website. See if your goal matches theirs and then make up your minds.' Pranav then gave them a few examples of what they might find if they looked up the RSS. They would find that a man who was a member of the RSS and was trained by them ended up killing Mahatma Gandhi in 1948. That they were the one organisation that sided with the British colonisers while the rest of the country was struggling for independence.

'Really? Then we don't want to join them,' the boys said, a little startled.

'No, I want you to go look them up first, and then make up your minds,' Pranav instructed them.

Many months later, the boys connected with Pranav again, by which time he had forgotten about the conversation. 'Sir, we did look up the RSS and decided not to join them. We registered our group separately.'

It was an exciting new space that Pranav now inhabited. But every now and then, some unresolved issue from his past flew in through the window and jangled his nerves. It caught unsuspecting colleagues by surprise when Pranav let off some steam now and then. On one occasion, a colleague was driving in her car with him. They were returning to the office from a meeting when a man in orange robes stopped them to ask for money. 'He was a sadhu type, you know, the kind of person who is clad in saffron and who loftily asks you for money, saying—You will be blessed if you donate some to me.' She was convulsed with laughter as she told the story. 'I refused the man politely three times, saying I didn't want to pay. Pranav was quiet the first two times. But when it happened the third time, he just blew his top. He yelled out of the car window, "Sisterfucker, just get out of here! You people just turn up here from UP and Bihar, you think all Gujaratis are fuckin' idiots who you can fool by just putting on some saffron clothes? Get out or I will come after you!"'

Within the office space, Pranav's response to similar provocation was more contained but still zealously applied. A colleague said that no one enforced the separation of religion from the work space quite as effectively as he did. She explained how a Muslim colleague had once asked Pranav during the month of Ramzan if there was a space where he could spread out his prayer mat. 'In an institutional space like this office, no religious marker either in the room or on your person is allowed. So you cannot offer your prayers here,' Pranav had replied and made an alternate suggestion. 'There is a public park just across the road. You could go there, and there would be no problem with that.' After the man left, Pranav turned to his co-worker and confidante and grinned. 'That's what I call killing two birds with one stone. I could have let him spread his prayer mat in a quiet corner in the office, but that public park is a place that the RSS has cornered to hold its shakhas. Let them see that it is in fact, a public place where Muslims can also come and offer prayers.' He laughed in his crazy way, eyebrows arched, thin frame shaking with the effort.

But there was an inner torment that Pranav hid well. Pranav's former boss said it was as if he was always challenging you in a way that was never expressed in words. 'This guy was full of dissent and full of politics. And that's what we needed.'

There was of course a price to pay for the transformation. Pranav explained it thus: 'You have to be prepared to leave your foundational relationships. And you also have to be ready to live with compromise. Because certain relationships you can't leave. Like your parents you can't leave, and if you are married, then your partner. A certain level of compromise which also doesn't hurt you much. Otherwise you won't be able to live with it.' Then he went completely silent. The fan whirred noisily.

'It takes a lot of pain,' he eventually continued. 'Reaching that state of compromise. Not the transformation but compromise. Or some kind of negotiation-based common ground. It takes a lot of time. A lot of pain. Which you have to be ready to invest in. It's worth it, because everyone starts to respect you. They see the transformation and they see the truth.'

The truth was hard for people closest to Pranav to accept. Like his parents, for instance. If they openly acknowledged that their rebellious son was right, it would mean accepting that much of what they believed or held on to was wrong. But they saw over time that the rebellion had come from a place of consideration, and had also gone someplace useful and important. There was a quiet, grudging acceptance after all these years that maybe their son wasn't completely worthless after all. Pranav saw the change and it made him indescribably happy when they started to consult him on family matters once again. They began to take his advice. He could belong again, without having to fit in.

'I know that now they respect me the most in the whole family, because in a situation of conflict, they go by what I say,' Pranav said, happily.

But in the end, coming to terms with all of this was a very lonely process, and Pranav realised that perhaps it would always be.

TWENTY-EIGHT

Dusk is a devious time. Hindu mythology says so, and Dungar was a believer. It was at dusk that Lord Vishnu had appeared on earth to defeat a demon who had been granted immortality by Lord Brahma, the creator. The demon was unstoppable. He could be defeated neither by day nor night, not by man or woman. So Vishnu appeared as Narasimha, half man and half lion, at twilight. The in-between time where anything was possible. Dungar was standing in the evening light, framed by the pink halo of this sun—half this, half that. He was always struggling with two selves in one. Tribal and non-tribal, Bhil and Hindu. Now, as he was about to deliver a speech, he needed those gathered to see only one half. His avatar as BJP campaigner. Minus the shadow of Keshubhai's party that he had used and dumped.

It was election time. Dungar wanted the village to see that he was back with the BJP as the same powerful leader who was once the head of the block, taluka pramukh. The sun was dipping in and out of the clouds like an orange sweet, staining the edges. Dungar had gathered a small group of people in the Dalit section of the village. He was flanked by two election assistants on their scooters. As people around him sat on their haunches, some rolling bidis, he said, 'Do any of you remember the thirteen-day government the BJP formed once upon a time?' The group stared at him blankly.

If this was going to be the start of a long sermon on history, they were tuning out. Dungar was trying to take them back to the time when the BJP government lasted less than two weeks to make the point that each person sitting there had the power to bring down a government in no time at all if they wanted. But he stopped. No one was here for the speech. One day before the election, all they wanted was their share of booze. No booze, no votes. That's how it had always been. His assistants opened the hatch under the seat of their scooters and took out tiny bottles, each holding a quarter of dark liquid that passed for whisky, smuggled in from Madhya Pradesh. The group got what they had come for.

For Dungar, the optics of this election mattered more than anything. He needed the BJP to see that he was back in their fold. His tribal rights organisation had secured a grant for a girls' hostel, which was running from his home. He had spent a tidy sum of money on it, and needed the schemes he had applied for to continue to be approved. If only that dreaded, destabilising self-doubt could be extinguished. If only he could be certain that no one would kick the pedestal out from under him. This was the downside of rising so fast. Losing perspective.

He had built five outdoor toilets for the girls and converted three rooms in his house into dormitories. Twenty girls from villages quite far away occupied them, their colourful metal trunks stacked in rows by their mattresses as they pored over textbooks and studied at the local school. To sustain this operation—the production of food on a giant scale twice a day, stacks of corn rotis and a kadhai full of tuar dal—the grants needed to keep coming. And the politics that drove it needed to be played. Dungar had to return to his exalted position of dispute-sorter, problem-solver and tallest

Hindu and tribal leader on the horizon. So he worked hard from election to election over the next few years, trying to rebuild himself.

The village panchayat election was the test for whether Dungar's currency as a political player was intact. The night before voting day, it was all down to the details. The time for posturing was over. The evening fix needed to get to each household on time. Dungar climbed up the ladder to the roof of his house to bring down a cardboard box hidden away from the children. It contained quart-sized bottles with a transparent glue-like liquid that was meant to be gin. Another packet had large bottles of the locally preferred cola drink, Thums Up. It was almost dark and time to go door to door. Two bottles per house for the two seats going to the polls—the district- and block-level representatives. There was a booze etiquette in place that Dungar was sticking to in his delivery. If a man was a regular hooch drinker or consumer of the locally extracted sap from the mahuda tree, he was given booze that was one grade higher—a bottle of gin. If a man was already a gin drinker, he got quarts of whisky—one grade above his regular consumption preference. A brand called King's Whisky, in this case. Women got bottles of Thums Up or Sprite. It was generally assumed that they did not drink alcohol.

The bottles had to be delivered before sundown, before the men had filled themselves with a dinner full of thick rotis with efficiently absorbent starch. That would make it impossible for the alcohol to deliver on its promise of getting people wasted. As soon as the bottles were delivered, they were downed in a few quick gulps. Halfway through the distribution, Dungar realised that the alco-math had gone wrong. He had fallen short. Quick damage control was required. A few phone calls, and forty more cases of liquor were supplied by the husband of the contesting woman candidate.

The night sky in the village shimmered with stars. It was time to visit a pre-election event being organised by a BJP supporter. The setting was full of pomp and show in a maidan with a colourful tent. At the back was a long and narrow carpet where hundreds of people sat in a row. They were served food laced with a request: to vote for the party that had sponsored the meal. A high-profile BJP member of parliament arrived, stepping out of his big white SUV, orange scarf around his neck and moustache waxed into upright position. Large speakers sounded bhajans and devotional songs that shattered the air with their tuneless high pitch. Dungar sat with the MP, a deferential smile in place.

A few hours later, when the MP had left and the last sleepy villager made his way out of the tent, Dungar's phone began to ring incessantly. A fight had broken out between BJP and Congress party supporters. Local elections were nothing if not a bloodfest. It all started when a Congress snoop had turned up for the evening's event uninvited, leading to a heated exchange. Dungar was called upon to play his part even though he was no longer an elected village representative. He was thrilled to see that the village still counted on him, and was more than happy to help. Everyone converged outside the hut of a former sarpanch. It was winter, and they squatted around a weak fire made up of dry sticks and leftover hay. It wasn't long before their anger was drowned by the last dregs of alcohol. The collective catharsis had a particularly orgiastic aftertaste. 'Sisterfucker,' said one, barely visible as the fire breathed its last. 'I will empty my dick right here,' said another amid laughter and the feeble crackling of twigs as the fire slowly extinguished itself. The next day, they voted for the BJP.

But Dungar's future with the party remained uncertain. His dual face had become an inconvenience. He realised he wasn't getting the same attention from the party anymore. If the BJP could not keep his position stable, he would have to look elsewhere. 'The wind was blowing against the BJP. I was a BJP-wala still, but I could say for sure that they were not going to do any good work here. They say a lot but do absolutely nothing,' Dungar said privately, away from the hectic electioneering.

But the party had eyes and ears everywhere, and they may have sniffed a dissenter. The shadow of someone shifty who had already moved away once. A party worker with a grudge. A long-time BJP worker who knew Dungar described him in a fond but patronising way. 'Dungar does good work for sure, but then you know how it is when people ask for a party ticket to contest and they don't get it, they slowly drop out of meetings and all, na.' Sitting in her brightly lit drawing room in a festive orange sari, she nodded thoughtfully.

Dungar was beginning to find out just how hard the road ahead was. Fortunately for him, dissent within the Sangh Parivar was gathering momentum across the state. Voices had begun to rise soon after the supreme leader of Gujarat, Narendra Modi, won the general elections in 2014 and became India's prime minister. He no longer had time to manoeuvre party politics in the state. It set many tongues wagging. Especially of people who were upset because power had not been shared with them.

No one was loyal any longer. Dungar calculated that perhaps it may not be such a bad thing to be a political juggler after all. Publicly he still canvassed for the BJP. Privately he started to fish around in other waters. His first stop was a regional party that barely had a presence in Gujarat but was looking to get a foot in the door. Dungar decided to help them in the next local election. It was time to do what he knew best. Scoop out the insides of one party and offer the innards as conquest to another. He convinced the BJP to appoint a candidate he was sure would lose, and simultaneously pulled out his bag of tricks for the opposition. But all that successful arithmetic did not give Dungar what he wanted. A secure foothold, a sense that all this would not just vanish.

The next year, there was another election. The candidate Dungar had publicly canvassed for from the BJP lost. In many parts of rural Gujarat, the Congress party was gaining ground. Dungar began to shift his gaze in that direction, but no doors seemed to be opening. Perhaps the double-game was wearing thin, and could not be repeated election after election. It was also tiring.

One afternoon, when Dungar had spent the day tending to his corn crop, he said, 'I am fed up of politics.' By now, the game was almost a second skin. Perhaps he needed to find a new way to play it. In one area of his life, though, Dungar did finally acquire the stability and comfort he was looking for. At home. After his first wife threatened to leave him and had to be talked out of a court case she had filed against him, he had left her and their three children. He paid them a maintenance and they lived with his parents, but Dungar had decided to start a whole new life. He built himself a grand white marble house on top of a hill and converted part of it into a hostel for tribal girls. Away from his former wife and kids, he decided it was time to restart his personal life.

In 2012, he got married again. It had all unfolded when Dungar started a school for girls and was looking for a teacher. A slender young tribal woman with long hair and a big, broad smile applied for the post, and Dungar fell in love. He gave her the job and married her. They had a baby girl with big round eyes and a button-shaped nose the following year. 'I want her to grow up and learn English. I want her to study well and get a job,' Dungar said as he put his daughter on his lap and tickled her face with her toy teddy. Three years later, they had a boy. Dungar was a proud and engaged parent this time around.

At the bottom of the hill, across from Dungar's new marble establishment, was the house of his father and brother, where his old wife lived with his three grown-up children. It was all there, right in front of him, whether he liked it or not—the life his father had forced on him. The life he was born into. Where he was still the slightly apologetic boy hiding in the body of a strong and confident man. Perhaps he would always have to be a bit of a juggler, balancing his old life with the new. Pieces of him split many ways, like his tribal-ness. Now Hindu, now not. Now Muslim baiter, now peacemaker. Always in the twilight zone, searching for one place to be.

TWENTY-NINE

For Suresh, darkness was an old friend. But he could never have imagined that the most humiliation he would ever face would be delivered by his wife. He stood facing her in the Ahmedabad family court, where she had filed for divorce on grounds of cruelty, rape and domestic violence. Suresh was searching for some sign that this could be undone. An expression on her face that said she still belonged to him. There was none. Farzana didn't look at him at all. Suresh cast a sideways glance at her. Then, seeing that she had not looked back at him, Suresh turned to the judge with his hands folded, body bent over in supplication. Tears rolled down his cheek as he choked over his words: 'Sir, please give me another date and a court-appointed lawyer. I don't have the ability to hire a private lawyer.' Then he broke down. 'I can't live without her, sir, we have two kids, they are fourteen and sixteen years old ...' he trailed off, convulsed with sobs.

Farzana stared at the ground. The judge set another date for the hearing. As she left the court, Farzana spotted their two children outside. Richie glared at her, then turned to her father and cried. Vivian didn't look at her at all. Suresh was whisked away by the police into a van that drove him back to Sabarmati jail.

Farzana dialled her mother desperately, her nose red from having cried privately in the court washroom. 'Ammi, where are you, please come quickly,' she said, her voice a little unsteady. Suresh's aunts and cousin and extended family from Chharanagar had come to court to boost his morale. They had encountered her outside the court and remarked, 'You've come alone? No one from your family came along?'—suggesting that she would not survive alone. She needed her mother to show them that her own family stood firmly by Farzana's side.

A few minutes later, Khatoonbibi arrived, waving frantically from the parking lot of the court. They hugged each other tight. And started to talk really fast. 'Ammi, you should have—' Farzana started to say and Khatoonbibi interrupted with, 'I know, Farzoo, I left my phone at home by mistake in all the panic.'

This was the last time Suresh would see even a flicker of emotion on his wife's face. Over the next two years, over many court hearings, he was mostly absent. On the two occasions that he did make an appearance, both he and Farzana wore their most impenetrable faces. Eyes of stone.

On Farzana's hands, there was evidence of impossible pain in three places where there were once love tattoos the two of them had made. She had laboriously scraped them off her skin by rubbing on powdered lime—a harsh reactive plaster normally used to paper over brick walls. The skin burned so sharply that it exposed the pink flesh underneath and rendered her arm stiff and useless with pain. Several weeks of treatment at a plastic surgeon's was needed to mend it. But Farzana was unrepentant. 'I did not want any physical reminder of Suresh on me at all. If it meant cutting off my arm, I'd do that.'

It was impossible to know what Suresh felt. But if the folklore narrated to Farzana by the extended network of

Chharanagar was anything to go by, then it seemed that, even for someone as volatile as him, the scars ran deep. Word got to Farzana that Suresh had put a garland around her photograph in their home in Chharanagar, symbolically declaring her dead.

The two children bore visible signs of distress. A few months before Farzana left Chharanagar, Vivian had erupted in a rage, just like his father. One evening, midway through a conversation with his sister and mother, he pulled out a large pair of scissors and moved the blades towards Farzana's face. His eyes were large and red, bulging out of their sockets, and language had given way to gibberish as the rage within him spiralled out of control. The arrival of a stranger caused a momentary interruption that saved Farzana and Richie's eyes from being taken out. Vivian put away the scissors.

The fight had ostensibly been about a subject Vivian was very sensitive about, being called effeminate. But the root of the anger lay in a cycle that was spun a generation ago. The highly toxic relationship between father and son. Suresh had been brought up on a diet of abuse from his father; 'He is not my son. I don't know who my wife slept with to produce him.' And he handed it to his son as inheritance. 'This is not my son,' Suresh would say when he saw Vivian play with dolls and hang out with his many girl friends. He suspected that his son was gay. When there was enough liquor in him, Suresh would proclaim loudly to the world, or whoever cared to listen, 'He's the son of a eunuch. Half Muslim. Chhakka. Kateyla miya.'

Their daughter Richie was her father's favourite. And that left its own kind of scars. The year her mother left Chharanagar, Richie ran away with a boy she had met at a local tattoo parlour. They almost copy-pasted Suresh and

Farzana's elopement by running away to another state—
to Maharashtra and the city of Mumbai. Then the boy's
parents lured them back with the promise that they would
let the couple be. Suresh was incensed that his daughter was
taken away by a man not of his choosing. His family filed a
complaint with the local police. Enraged and upset, Richie
visited her father in his jail cell, hoping to win him over and
get him to approve of her choice. He instructed his chachi
to break up the love affair instead. A distraught Richie went
running to her mother for help. She hoped that Farzana would
keep her and her lover, and eventually get them married.

But Farzana was living in a one-room tenement with her
mother and brother and his family. There was no space to
accommodate Richie. Farzana told her daughter to return
to Chharanagar and stay with Suresh's family. It left Richie
feeling doubly abandoned. She burst into tears. 'What kind
of mother are you?' she screamed at Farzana, her eyes large
and swollen.

Richie spent the next couple of years in torment, swinging
wildly between hating and loving her parents. Some of the
time, she called her mother an irresponsible slut. Then she
calmed down, reached out to Farzana and told her what a
brave and good parent she was. She came to a resting point
when she found another lover. This time it looked like a happy
match. They were married. Richie made sure she displayed
the wedding pictures on Facebook. Her red wedding lehenga
framed in gold embroidery, wrists covered with red and white
bridal bangles. She also declared proudly that she had found
her vocation. She was a model and was in demand for more
than a few photo shoots. Crucially, her marriage and work
allowed her to successfully move out of Chharanagar.

Of all the women whose lives Suresh had destroyed, it

was Farzana who lived to tell her tale, both in court and outside it. But the trauma took its toll. There were moments of such unbearable pain that she ran out of her home in Jamalpur to throw herself off the nearest flyover. And then the voices in her head would come to an abrupt stop. Perhaps the interruption was as simple and mundane as the traffic sounds from below, or maybe it was a force within.

She would walk back home, eyes swollen, and tell her mother a lie. 'I had a fever, Ammi, and I took two pills instead of one, so my face is like this.' Her mother would nod, the heaviness too much for either of them to acknowledge.

Over the months, her trips to the flyover became less frequent. In fact, a year after living apart from Suresh, Farzana felt much less oppressed by memories of him. On most mornings, she was bent over a pot of hot oil, frying slivers of crescent-shaped chicken spleen and liver, or kaleji, in a spicy red coriander-and-chilli paste, for her new venture. A food cart that she had set up right outside her home. Also on offer were fried curly papads—long barrel-shaped ones, tiny circular ones in green, yellow and pink—and greasy deep-fried chicken lollies and crisp keema samosas, all arranged in neat piles on the cart. Three pieces of kaleji at Rs 10. Four samosas for Rs 20. There was sweat on her brow and a twinkle in her eye. One day, her lorry would turn into a restaurant. She had a dream.

THIRTY

18 December 2017 was a strange day in the life of Gujarat. Not nearly as strange as 28 February 2002. But as days go, this one wore a peculiar face. It was counting day in the life of yet another election. And the BJP had tried its best to lull voters into a stupor. In which the memory of 2002 and the violence and blood, pain and tears were to be erased like it never happened. It had been fifteen years since the violence of 2002. So, the BJP built its campaign on a tower of forgetting. However, when the results trickled in on 17 December, it was clear that people still remembered.

It made Pranav's wiry frame shake with laughter when the BJP blew victory bugles. They had won by a whisker. But rural Gujarat had voted overwhelmingly against the party. And it was clear that nobody was forgetting anything in a hurry. The wheels had turned for the BJP and its extended arm in the Sangh Parivar precisely because they had taken their fantasies as far as they could, and in Gujarat, it seemed as if there was no more room for the hate to grow.

As the results poured in, Pranav carried out his election ritual. Which was to get out of the state and drink till the show was done. It was just as well, since he had made the unravelling of the Sangh Parivar's politics his business: provoking people he worked with and trained never to forget their recent history, or what it was like to have shaped it. Every recounting felt like a stab wound. But the wound was an essential antidote. The best counter to the violence and fear and the loss of self was in the remembering. In the pain and anguish and uncertainty it brought with it. But always, the remembering.

ॐ

The night before voting day in the 2017 election, Dungar was crouched over a meagre fire with drunken neighbours and voters from his village. He had just finished making his umpteenth speech about how the BJP was a party of hollow men. He was trying this time to help the Congress win. His father mocked this double-game. Bent over the fire, sucking on a roughly rolled tobacco joint, the father said, 'I will vote for the BJP and only the BJP till my dying day.' Dungar tried to hide his hurt pride with his best fake grin. The fire slowly went out, leaving only the village sky, dark and infinite. After all this time, fifteen years on from having been the nervous tribal boy with no face, here he was—wealthier, much respected, but still a little lost. Still his father's boy.

ॐ

Suresh's total withdrawal from all forms of communication other than violence spoke for him. Much louder than anything he could ever say. A reminder and an embarrassment to all those who lived through 2002 that this too was part of their dream. The nightmares that came with fulfilling their fantasies of silencing the other. The most inconvenient part of that success.

The people who had sent Suresh to jail for his crimes—people like Abdul Majid, who had lost nine members of his family in 2002—were tired. They were tired of being asked to tell the story of their victimhood over and over again. They had just one thing to tell those who came around asking for more stories. 'Don't look at us. We're done talking. Look at them.'

AFTERWORD

It may seem profoundly foolish in the end to try and tell the story of a mob through the lives of only three random individuals. However, as I met between fifty and hundred people accused variously of participating in the crimes of 2002, I realised that a larger canvas of stories was impossible. Most people were not open to telling their stories of hate, guilt and complicity. They were fighting court cases, or had simply decided this is not what they wanted. It took ten years, in fact, for me to convince the first of the three people in this book to let me tell his story. Even then, the interviews were spread out over three years with long gaps in the middle where he would not speak because it was too traumatic to go over that time again. The three stories I confined this book to are the ones that revealed themselves to me in all their layers and complexity. They are neither geographically nor demographically representative of the whole.

They are intimate, however, and that I have hoped provides a different way of seeing. Distance keeps us comfortable. Getting up close is unsettling because we have to step into the shoes of the mob and feel what it's like to be one of them. That's when these stories are no longer about those people out there doing incomprehensible things. They might allow us to have conversations that cut through the amnesia, the denial around 2002 and its actors. A denial that has engulfed us all.

ACKNOWLEDGEMENTS

This book is a collaborative effort. It could not have happened but for at least 200 specific people that I must acknowledge and thank, and I want to say with all the humility I can muster—I am truly shaken and altered by the faith reposed in me.

One hundred and five people funded this book. When I ran out of research funds, these friends and friends of friends and acquaintances and strangers from all over the world responded to my fundraising campaign. I crowdfunded half the money spent in the research and writing. The campaign was meant to run for forty-five days but I raised more than my target: 9.8 lakh rupees in fifteen days flat. All 105 of you—you overwhelm me. While I was losing my father to cancer, it is the faith all of you put in me that told me this book must be done.

I've put all your names down alphabetically at the end of this section because if I did what I really wanted to—write a line about each of you—that would be a book in itself and my publisher would quite possibly kill me.‡

I would like to thank K. Ravi for spending a day at the farm filming the crowdfunding video for free, because he is a friend and because he believed in the book. For the same reasons, Nandu and everyone at Flamingo Films gave me their equipment for free. Thank you. Also to my dear friend Hitesh Kumar, Hemkant, Ayush and everyone at Splat Studios for allowing me to edit the film there. Everyone at Kalakar, Savneet and his team at Webcurry that helped Neanderthal me create the web page. And Sondeep Shankar, Yashas Chandra, Hans

Aanki, Sonali Ghosh, Charles Marquand, Richard Eaton, Razim Ozan Kutahyali and Mahmood Mamdani for allowing me to carry their writing and photographs on 'The Anatomy of Hate' website as part of the crowdfunding exercise.

The book-shaped monster that swallowed me whole over the last four years was all sorts of other things when I started out. At one time, I was considering making a documentary film, and at another it was supposed to be the cover story for *Tehelka* magazine, where I fell out with the editor over it. So I asked her if I could get a second opinion, which is when I met the person who is chiefly responsible for seeding the idea of a book—Professor Ashis Nandy. As he scratched his beard and bent over his desk at the Centre for the Study of Developing Societies, he said, 'Forget the magazine story. This is worth at least a monograph.'

But before the book and the film and everything else, there was Pranav. A chance meeting with him all those years ago in 2004, while filming a TV story, changed everything. He made me see violence in a completely new way. So, dost, thank you for being you and allowing me to interview you at such length and for opening up about your life the way you have. Dungar—for teaching me so much about politics and the shape of all fears, and for hosting me in his lovely home through it all. And Farzana for being bold and brave and showing me the most terrifying side of this story. A ginormous thank you, Salimbhai, for your crucial inputs. This could not be written without you. And all of Suresh's victims and the people who grew up with him. Faridaben, Abdul Majidbhai and so many others—over thirty of you.

Thank you to Professor Ganesh Devy, my first point of contact in the world of Chharanagar. To Dakxin Chhara, Roxy Gagdekar, Kushal Batunge and many other people in both Chharanagar and Naroda Patiya whom I cannot name so they remain safe, but who have been absolutely vital to the book. To Shabana Mansuri for fighting Farzana's cases and mine endlessly, with no money but all the grit and determination that makes you such a fine lawyer and steadfast friend.

To Rajiv Pathak and Mahashweta—thank you for being wonderful friends, for letting me live in your lovely home for nearly three years and for allowing me to call you for all kinds of contacts, advice and perspective when I needed it.

And to my crazy and tightly-knit Gujarat family—Natvar Parmar, Beka Bekor and the ghost of Pranav Joshi. He left us some years ago but his laughter rings in my ears even now.

And my old friend turned new, turned old again and source of warmth and fun in Gujarat—Mandakini Kumari. And Chayaben for being an integral part of my life and home in Gujarat.

To Gaganbhai, Gagan Sethi, and to Vijay Parmar, who guided me through the madness and maze and search for the main protagonists of this book. Avni Sethi for being a friend and for hosting me as the very first writer in residence at the Conflictorium. To Baa, Amit, Shefali, Diwakar and everyone at the Conflictorium whose lives I made impossible while I lived there.

To Mukhtarbhai whose crucial leads guided me through much of my research. And whose humour requires another book to capture.

And to Tridip Surhud and Harmony Siganporia, with whom crucial conversations made me see Gujarat from the inside out.

To Radha Roy and Ingrid Srinath whose invaluable advice gave me the impetus to move to Gujarat. And to Richard Eaton for conversations over email and in person that have been soul food. The same goes for Mitch Crites and also Gurcharan Das.

To Rukmini Kumar, dear, dear friend who commissioned this book and introduced me to the person whom I have come to absolutely adore. My publisher V.K. Karthika who has held up my sky and protected me like I was a big, frisky cat in her home. That's the only way I can describe the impossible affection I feel for you, Karthika! To Ajitha, who turned many clumsy, tedious drafts into something worthy of printing. You are a magician. And to Vishwajyoti Ghosh—I drove you insane with utterly ridiculous ideas about the hardback cover, despite which you made the striking art that holds the book in place.

To Shikha Trivedy for introducing me to everything and everyone when I was a clueless reporter in Gujarat a decade and a half ago. Those connections led me to this place.

To Ayesha Kagal—friend, philosopher, guide—who saw an abominable first draft and poured so much love into it, line by line and word by word, that it forced me to remove my blinkers and write properly. I love you, Ayesha. Go turn red.

And Vani—for also bravely powering through this first draft. You are one heck of a friend.

To Jatin—with whom I have gone over every micro-minuscule detail of the book. Thank you for being there through all the emotional outbursts and heartache that, as my closest friend, you absorbed over many, many rounds of alcohol and dinner. We've literally drunk our way through this, so it's your book as much as it's mine!

To Charles—my other dear, dear friend whose gentle and firm perspective made me rewrite a very clunky draft. And who listened patiently to outpouring after outpouring, sticking back pieces of me that kept falling apart.

To Chulbul and Gunjan for crazy, stupid love and for fixing me with it so I could carry on. And Baloo Bear and Shambhavi, for the love and the technicolour dream coats we wear whenever we meet. To Shubhra for taking me to the hills with you and helping me unshackle myself from old book drafts. And for your infinite love. I love you right back! And to Shailan and Indrani Parker for letting me write in their lovely hillside home in Bhowali.

To the absolutely fabulous chaddi buddies who have been there, done that and some. Who have seen me through the most difficult times and put up with unforgivable behaviour that is hidden from the reader as I put on my best hat to write. Vani,

Nevi, Amrita, Shefali, Damini, Bijoya, Sonali, Shruti, Sarah, Nazli and Vivs: you guys are my rock, my strength, the place I laugh from. And also Neha, Mandy, Raksha, Heidi, Vasanthi, Anshula, Sid P., Soli, Sylvano, Gunjan J., Hitesh, Megha C., Anchal, Tilo, Jaya B., Avantika, Jaya and Gautam, Aashish, Payal and Bunny. To my childhood friends Ranjit Raina and Yamini Pande whose faith and constant online and offline support has been a great source of strength.

To all the women scribes I am so proud to be a kin of— the Network of Women in Media, India, and Rajeshwari in particular. I will never forget how you were on the phone constantly with me when I was under attack.

To my tapori gang—my other family, formerly the children of Tara Homes, now grown-up dudes. Sidhu, Siddhanth, Sunil, Rakesh, Ramu, Suman, Suraj, Afrez, Ifrez, Jaan, Javed, Asif and all the rest who are still at Tara. I love you all to bits.

To my brother Raghav and sister-in-law Charu for being there in the most trying circumstances and letting me literally sponge off them while I wrote.

To my cousin Vandana and her husband Saras and to the two pixies who are my chief advisers on all things from my exponentially increasing girth to the art of storytelling—Aditi and Abheek. And Romi, for his therapeutic licks and big wet spaniel nose.

To Ram Kewal, Chedilal, Ram Murti, Harbatti and Ved Prakash who work on our large sprawling farm. They took up all the slack on the grinding everyday tasks as I turned into a complete sloth through the writing of this book. Thank you all for your used before patience.

And to Chiku, Golu, Piloo and Munni. Woof and wooooooh right back.

Most of all, to the two people that are my sun, moon and entire universe. My mother, my gravitational force, and the reason I have any imagination and humanity at all. And my nephew Agastya, Gus, who wasn't even a thought when I first started work on this book, and is now three-going-on-thirty-three and the light of my life. A lot would be missing in these pages if it weren't for Gus rolling his 'gween' car and his many Lightning McQueens over my head.

Lastly, Pa. I lost you halfway through the making of this book, but you are still the centrifugal force within me. My inspiration and gut. Am pulling your beard as you look in here from that funny otherworldly place where you're stirring the pot, no doubt. I love you.

ৡ

‡ The 105 of you who crowdfunded this book! Thank you, thank you, thank you! Some of you wished to remain anonymous. I am sending you a private hug publicly.

1. Aamana Singh
2. Abbas Shamel Rizvi
3. Aditi and Brian Saxton
4. Amrita Tripathi
5. Anjum Rajabali
6. Ankit Gupta
7. Ankita Chawla
8. Ansh Verma
9. Arati Singh
10. Asha Agarwal
11. Avni Sethi
12. Ayesha Kagal
13. Bilal Zaidi
14. Bina Sarkar Ellias
15. Blaze Arizanov Kaspian
16. Brendan D. de Caires
17. Carmen Kagal
18. Charu Shankar and Raghav Laul
19. Damini Sinha
20. Dattaprasad Godbole

21. Debbie and James Thompson
22. Deepa Kamath
23. Deepan Thiagu
24. Ekta Sahni
25. Garima Jain
26. Gopalan T.N.
27. Gunjan Jain
28. Heidi Lipsanen
29. Husain Akbar
30. Ishan Prakash
31. Jatin Gupta
32. Javed Jafri
33. Jaya and Gautam Babbar
34. Laxmi Murthy
35. Kevin Oakley
36. Madhusudan
37. Mahesh Mathai
38. Mandira Nayar
39. Megha Chhabra
40. Melodika Sadri
41. Mitch Crites
42. Mirai Chatterjee
43. Nandini Ray
44. Nilima and Durgesh Shankar
45. Pradeep Bhat
46. Prashant Sareen
47. Preeti Sharma
48. Priyanka Borpujari
49. Priyanka Sharma Sindhar
50. Rachna Singh
51. Rakesh Shukla
52. Ranjit Raina
53. Ravish Kumar
54. Rini Simon Khanna

55. Ritu Saini
56. Rohit Sakunia
57. Rubina Jasani
58. Sarbani Bandyopadhyay
59. Saurabh Vishwakarma
60. Shayne Singh
61. Sheen S.B.
62. Shikha Trivedy
63. Shruti Dev
64. Shubhra Chaturvedi
65. Soli J. Sorabjee
66. Sonali Ghosh
67. Sonia and Ajai Shukla
68. Subodh Gupta
69. Suchet Malhotra
70. Sukruta Alluri
71. Surabhi Vaya
72. Swati Maheshwari
73. Tusha Mittal
74. Varun Narain
75. Vikram Baluja
76. Yamini Pande
77. Yashas Chandra
78. Yuman Hussain